*To Debby
Best r you!
B?*

I'LL BE SHORT

ALSO BY ROBERT B. REICH

The Future of Success

Locked in the Cabinet

The Work of Nations

Tales of a New America

The Resurgent Liberal

The Power of Public Ideas (editor)

New Deals (coauthored with John Donahue)

The Next American Frontier

I'LL BE SHORT

Essentials
for a
Decent
Working
Society

ROBERT B. REICH

Beacon Press
Boston

Beacon Press
25 Beacon Street
Boston, Massachusetts 02108-2892
www.beacon.org

Beacon Press books
are published under the auspices of
the Unitarian Universalist Association of Congregations.

Printed in the United States of America

07 06 05 04 03   8 7 6 5 4 3 2 1

This book is printed on acid-free paper that meets
the uncoated paper ANSI/NISO specifications
for permanence as revised in 1992.

Text design by Dan Ochsner

Composition by Wilsted & Taylor Publishing Services

Library of Congress Cataloging-in-Publication Data
Reich, Robert B.
I'll be short : essentials for a decent working society / Robert B. Reich.
p.   cm.
ISBN 0-8070-4340-0 (cloth : alk. paper)
ISBN 0-8070-4341-9 (pbk.)
1. Political planning—United States.   2. United States—Politics and
government—2001–   I. Title.
JK468.P64 R44   2002
320.973′01′1—dc21
2002003943

CONTENTS

PREFACE

It is far too early to know what historians will see when they look back on the years 2000 to 2002 from their perches in the future, but it's likely they will chronicle a profound change in America. The years leading up featured almost breathless excitement about getting rich quick in dot-coms, irrational exuberance in the stock market, and boundless confidence about the nation's power and place in the world. Then, in rapid succession, the dot-com bubble burst, the economy drifted into recession, and terrorists attacked with a deadliness and ferocity never known or even imagined before. Then one of our most successful corporations suddenly imploded, revealing a sham of accounting gimmicks and regulatory lapses; investors and employees lost big while top executives walked off with fortunes.

What have we learned, other than humility? We remain a blessedly optimistic people. But these two years have shaken our certainty about some things we had begun to take for granted—especially, I think, the idea that each of us can make it solely on our own. The get-rich-quick exuberance of the late nineties may have temporarily blinded us to how dependent we are on one another. Subsequent events serve as reminders that the strength of our economy and the security of our society rest on the bonds that connect us. But what, specifically, are these bonds? What do we owe one another as members of the same society?

This is a small book about these large questions. Some of the observations recorded here are culled from my writing during these fitful years. In collecting and fitting them together, my hope is to reveal a larger perspective on what is at stake and what we can do about it.

One of my themes concerns politics, and the heightened importance now of a politically active and engaged citizenry. As this volume goes to press, I am heeding my own advice in the extreme by running for governor of Massachusetts. By the time you get around to reading it, I may have succeeded— or else have returned to the far safer ground of commenting from the sidelines. If it's the former, I hope I can put some of those principles into action; if the latter, I hope others will.

CHAPTER ONE

Whatever Happened to the Social Contract?

Not since World War II have Americans felt so unified. We're fighting a war against terrorism and we're fighting to get the economy moving again. And we're all in this together. Except when it comes to paying the bill.

Add the cost of fighting the war to the biggest military buildup in two decades and extra security at home, and you're talking real money—hundreds of billions of dollars over the next few years. The Bush administration has also enacted a mammoth tax cut—$1.35 trillion over the next ten years. At this writing, the president is proposing almost $600 billion in additional cuts in income taxes and capital-gains taxes. The bulk of these cuts—those already enacted and those proposed—benefit large corporations and people who are already wealthy.

So who's going to pay? Take a guess. Middle- and lower-income Americans.

Most Americans now pay more in payroll taxes than they do in income taxes. Payroll taxes include Social Security and Medicare payments. You pay these taxes on the first $80,000 or so of your income (the ceiling rises slightly every year). After that you're home free. Bill Gates stops paying payroll taxes at a few minutes past midnight on January 1 every year.

None of the enacted or proposed tax cuts affect payroll taxes, even temporarily. To the contrary, they increase the odds that payroll taxes will have to be hiked. That's because the tax cuts, combined with the military buildup, will drain so much money out of the Treasury that there won't be enough money to pay for Social Security and Medicare by the time the early baby boomers begin retiring, about a decade from now. So payroll taxes probably will have to rise in order to fill the gap.

Get it? Income and capital-gains tax cuts for the rich now, payroll tax hikes on middle- and lower-income Americans to come.

Americans like to think we're all in this together, but the fact is that the economic fallout from terrorism is hitting some Americans much harder than others. When the slowdown began, layoffs and pay cuts hit hardest at manufacturing workers, white-collar managers, and professionals. Since the terrorist attacks, a different group is experiencing the heaviest job losses: the low-paid. Many are service workers in retail stores, restaurants, hotels, or other tourist-industry businesses that have been hard hit. Others are caregivers—social workers, hospital workers, elder-care workers—whose jobs and wages are on the line as public budgets are trimmed. The economy may be rebounding, but these people aren't.

Government is less helpful this time around. Safety nets are in tatters. Welfare-to-work programs made sense when work was plentiful, but without work, those no longer eligible for welfare have nowhere else to turn. Even job losers who still qualify find that welfare payments in most states are worth less than before.

Unemployment insurance is also harder for them to get. Since part-time workers, temps, the self-employed, and people who have moved in and out of employment often don't qualify, a large portion of the lower-wage workforce is excluded. Many who don't qualify are women with young children.

Meanwhile, federal programs for job training and low-income housing have been shrunk by budget cuts. State and local governments are in no position to step in. They're already strapped by rapidly declining tax revenues. Rather than beefing up social services, they're cutting them. Rather than improving our schools by reducing class size and offering all-day kindergartens and after-school programs, they're paring back. Instead of making higher education more affordable, it's getting out of reach for many families. Meanwhile, more Americans are in danger of losing health care or are paying more for the care they get.

In short, the fat years of the nineties left us woefully unprepared for a slower economy that's taking a particularly large toll on hardworking families and the poor.

In the past, when Americans faced a common problem—the Depression, a hot war, a cold war—we understood intuitively that we were all in it together. Someone's misfortune could be anyone's: "There but for the grace of God go I." Social insurance was a natural impulse, a first cousin to patriotism. It was not difficult to sense mutual dependence and to agree on a set of responsibilities shared by all members, exacting certain sacrifices for the common good.

But that sense of commonality is endangered as we drift into separate worlds of privilege and insecurity. I can't help asking, if you'll pardon me for questioning our newfound unity, whatever happened to the social contract?

The sobering news is that even our ten years of economic expansion didn't do much for the bottom half. Sure, they had jobs, but they had jobs before the last recession, too. The fact is, the median wage—the real take-home pay of the worker smack in the middle of the earnings ladder—is not much higher than it was in 1989. In my home state of Massachusetts, the typical household ended the roaring nineties $4,700 poorer (adjusted for inflation) than it began. And health and pension benefits for the bottom half continue to shrivel.

Many families have made up for the steady decline by working longer hours. The average middle-income married couple with children works almost 4,000 hours a year for pay—about seven weeks more than in 1990. But for most mortals who do not relish what they do for pay, more hours at work does not translate into a higher standard of living. On top of that, jobs are less secure. Health care is more expensive. Working families are shelling out huge bucks for good child care. And if you've got elderly parents who also need help, it's even rougher. At the same time, the upper reaches of America have never had it so good. Their pay and benefits have continued to rise.

Look, I don't begrudge anyone a fat paycheck or a big dividend check. But the worrier in me won't let go. I don't want my boys to grow up in a two-tiered society where they'll have to live in gated communities. Yet that's the direction we're heading in.

The problem is not that some of us are getting rich. That's the good news. The problem is that most of us are getting nowhere, even though we're working harder than ever before. We are hurtling toward a society composed of a minority who are profiting from changes in the economy and a majority who are not.

The consequence of this erosion extends beyond economics. It helps explain why hard-pressed parents can't find the time to raise their kids the way they themselves were raised and to pass on the values they grew up with; why voters whose family budgets pinch so tightly are outraged about government inefficiency and waste; why even instinctively generous Americans find their compassion toward the less fortunate flagging; why our politics have become so angry, even sometimes ugly.

Perhaps most important are the moral consequences. Put simply, it just isn't right. The glaring, grotesque wrongness of what's happening to hardworking American families spawns despair and cynicism. It affronts our values, mocking the American bargain linking effort and reward. It makes people feel like suckers and gnaws away at the precious ethic of responsibility. It closes the gate to the very poor. Ultimately, the hollowing-out of the middle class and the creation of a two-tiered society pose a mortal threat to what's always been special about our country.

Why isn't this being talked about? My guess is that Republicans don't feel comfortable with the topic because they don't have any solutions they'd find palatable. The right wing of the Democratic party has drifted toward a flaccid Republicanism, where the basic philosophy is that everyone is on his or her own. Corporate America isn't particularly eager to talk about it, or to sponsor television programs or advertise in magazines that do. But the fact is, as we proceed with the war on terrorism, our domestic agenda is in shambles. We need to make the case that we can only be a strong nation if the working middle class and the less fortunate are brought along. True national security begins with economic security.

Millions of Americans—myself included—were raised to believe in a simple bargain: Anybody who worked hard could earn a better life for themselves and their family. That's *anybody*—not just the wellborn, not just the well connected. Anybody with the drive and discipline to make the most of their opportunities had a decent chance to make it. Corporate America backed the bargain, too. Employees who worked hard and gave it their all could share in the company's success. If the company did well, their jobs were reasonably secure, and their wages and benefits rose.

In the 1950s, my mother and father worked six days a week in their small clothing shop, selling skirts and dresses to the wives of factory workers. I remember making signs when they had special sales: COTTON DRESSES, $2.99; BLOUSES,

$1.00. As factory wages went up, local families had a bit more to spend every year, and my parents' little business grew less precarious. They went upscale. We all did better together. Growing together was the way it worked in America.

America has got off that track. We're growing apart—and at a quickening pace. My parents retired before the new economy elbowed out the old. Most of those factory jobs are now gone. Jobs like them accounted for over a third of all American jobs in the 1950s; now, fewer than 16 percent. Many of the old service jobs have disappeared as well. Telephone operators have been replaced by automated switching equipment, bank tellers by automated teller machines, gas station attendants by self-service pumps that accept credit cards, and secretaries by computers and voice mail. Any job that can be done more cheaply by a computer is now gone, or pays far less than before.

We can't bring back the old economy, and shouldn't try. But that doesn't leave us helpless. What we can do is create a new economy in which many more succeed.

Earnings began splitting between the have-mores and the have-lesses largely because of two revolutions—one in computer technology, the other in global economic integration. The combined effect has been to shift demand in favor of workers with the right education and skills to take advantage of these changes, and against workers without them. Meanwhile, the unionized segment of the workforce has shrunk. Today, fewer than 10 percent of private-sector employees are unionized. In 1955, 35 percent were unionized. At the same time, the real value of the minimum wage has declined. The drop in unionization has taken a toll on the wages of men without college degrees. The drop in the minimum wage has taken the biggest toll on the wages of working women without college degrees.

The real puzzle is why in recent years we've let this happen. If the right education and skills are so important, why haven't we done more for our schools? Why is the federal government cutting back on job training? Why is college becoming less affordable? If family incomes are under greater and greater stress, why have we let unions wither and the minimum wage decline? Why haven't we widened the circle of prosperity so that more Americans have a decent shot at it? In short, why has the social contract come undone? In the world's preeminent democratic-capitalist society, one might have expected just the reverse: As the economy grew through technological progress and global integration, the "winners" from this process would compensate those who bore the biggest burdens, and still come out far ahead. Rather than being weakened, the social contract would be strengthened.

Nations are not passive victims of economic forces. Citizens can, if they so choose, assert that their mutual obligations extend beyond their economic usefulness to one another, and act accordingly. Throughout our history the United States has periodically asserted the public's interest when market outcomes threatened social peace—curbing the power of the great trusts, establishing pure food and drug laws, implementing a progressive federal tax, imposing a forty-hour workweek, barring child labor, creating a system of social security, expanding public schooling and access to higher education, extending health care to the elderly, and so forth. We did part of this through laws, regulations, and court rulings, and part through social norms and expectations about how we wanted our people to live and work productively together. In short, this nation developed and refined a strong social contract, which gave force to the simple proposition that prosperity could include almost everyone.

Every society and culture possesses a social contract—sometimes implicit, sometimes spelled out in detail, but usually a mix of both. The contract sets out the obligations of members of that society toward one another. Indeed, a society or culture is *defined* by its social contract. It is found within the pronouns "we," "our," and "us." *We* hold these truths to be self-evident; *our* peace and freedom is at stake; the problem affects all of *us*. A quarter of a century ago, when the essential provisions of the American social contract were taken for granted by American society, there was hardly any reason to state them. Today, as these provisions wither, they deserve closer scrutiny.

To the extent that there's been a moral core to American capitalism, it's consisted of three promises.

First, as companies did better, their employees would too. As long as a company was profitable, employees knew their jobs were secure. When profits rose, wages and benefits (health care and pensions) rose, too. In harder times, companies accepted lower profits to retain their workers. At worst, if a recession hit hard, companies laid workers off temporarily and then hired them back as soon as the economy turned up. The communities where most employees lived were also part of the contract: As long as the company was profitable, it remained in the community—often underwriting charities and responding to community needs.

"The job of management," proclaimed Frank Abrams, chairman of Standard Oil of New Jersey, in a 1951 address typical of the era, "is to maintain an equitable and working balance among the claims of the various directly interested groups . . . stockholders, employees, customers, and the public at large. Business managers are gaining in professional status partly because they see in their work the basic responsibilities [to the public] that other professional men have long recognized in theirs."

The second provision of the social contract was that working people were paid enough to support themselves and their families. No family with a full-time worker would be in poverty. If there weren't any jobs or if the breadwinner was disabled or had died, the family would be kept out of poverty through social insurance. The nation instituted unemployment insurance, Social Security for the elderly and disabled, aid to widows, which became Aid to Families with Dependent Children, and Medicare and Medicaid. "From the cradle to the grave," said Franklin Roosevelt, "people ought to be in a social insurance system."

We never quite got there, of course. And Roosevelt failed

to recognize that handouts can have negative side effects, such as deterring some people from trying to fend for themselves, or inducing some wealthy retirees to regard Social Security as an absolute entitlement. Still, for most of the next half century, most Americans agreed that people who worked hard or wanted to work hard, and nonetheless fell on their faces, should be helped out.

The third provision of the social contract: Everyone should have an opportunity fully to develop his or her talents and abilities through publicly supported education. The national role in education began in the nineteenth century with the Morrill Act, establishing land grant colleges. In the early decades of the twentieth century a national movement swept across America to create free education through the twelfth grade for every young person. After the Second World War, the GI Bill made college a reality for millions of returning veterans. Other young people gained access to advanced education through a vast expansion of state-subsidized public universities and community colleges. In the 1950s our collective conscience, embodied in the Supreme Court, finally led us to resolve that all children, regardless of race, must have the same—not separate—educational opportunities.

It is important to understand what this social contract was and what it was not. It defined our sense of fair play, but it was not primarily about redistributing wealth. There would still be the rich and the poor in America. The contract merely proclaimed that at some fundamental level we were all in it together, that as a society we depended on one another. The economy could not prosper unless vast numbers of employees had more money in their pockets. None of us could be economically secure unless we shared the risks of economic life. A better-educated workforce was in all our interests.

But the social contract is unraveling. Profitable companies no longer offer job security. Now they routinely downsize their workforces, or resort to what might be called "down-waging" and "down-benefiting." The term "layoff" no longer means what it used to—most are now permanent, not temporary. We need a new word to describe the new phenomenon. Perhaps we should call them "castoffs." Companies are replacing full-time workers with independent contractors, temporary workers, and part-timers. They're bringing in younger workers at lower wage scales to replace older workers with higher pay, or are subcontracting the work to smaller firms offering lower wages and benefits. Employer-provided health benefits are declining across the board, and health costs are being shifted to employees in the form of higher copayments, deductibles, and premiums. Defined-benefit pension plans are giving way to 401(k) plans with little or no employer contributions. About half of workers on private payrolls have no employer-sponsored retirement plan at all.

Meanwhile, beginning in the early 1980s, American companies battled against unionization with more ferocity than at any time in the previous half-century. The incidence of companies illegally firing their employees for trying to organize unions (adjusted for the number of certification elections and union voters) increased from 14 percent in the late 1970s to 32 percent in the early 1980s, where it more or less remained. This is one part of the reason why the unionized portion of the private-sector workforce has plummeted.

The drive among American companies to reduce their labor costs is understandable, given that payrolls constitute 70 percent of the cost of doing business, and that pressures on companies to cut costs and show profits have intensified. Competition is more treacherous in this new economy, where large size and low unit costs no longer guarantee a competitive advantage, and where institutional investors demand instant performance. Yet it is also the case that the compensation of senior management, professional, and highly skilled technical workers has escalated in recent years. In large companies, top executive compensation increased throughout the 1990s at the rate of over 10 percent per year, after inflation.

Top executives and their families receive ever more generous health benefits, and their pension benefits are soaring in the form of compensation deferred until retirement. Although they have no greater job security than others, when they lose their jobs it is not uncommon for them to receive "golden parachutes" studded with diamonds. The specter of Enron executives making off with the company jewels while employees' savings disappear is only the latest and most extreme example.

The second provision—a job paying enough to keep a family out of poverty, and social insurance when no job is available—is also breaking down. The real value of the minimum wage is now some 20 percent below its value in the late 1970s. Unemployment insurance isn't adequate for people permanently laid off and in need of a new job. It was designed for temporary layoffs during dips in the business cycle. And it doesn't cover the ever-growing number of workers who are employed part-time, or who move from job to job. For those not covered by unemployment insurance and threatened with destitution, welfare has traditionally offered an alternative. But even before welfare "reform" eliminated that safety net in 1996, welfare payments were shrinking in many states.

In fact the entire idea of social insurance is under attack. Proposals are being floated for the wealthier and healthier to opt out. Whether in the form of private "medical savings accounts" to replace Medicare, or "personal security accounts" to replace Social Security, the effect would be much the same: The wealthier and healthier would no longer share the risk with those who have a higher probability of being sicker or poorer.

The third part of the social contract, access to a good education, is also under severe strain. The federal government accounts for only eight cents of every public dollar spent on primary- and secondary-school education in the United States; states and localities divide the rest. As Americans increasingly segregate by level of income into different townships, local tax bases in poorer areas cannot support the quality of schooling available to the wealthier. Public expenditures per pupil are significantly lower in school districts in which the median household income is less than $20,000 than they are in districts where the median household income is $50,000 or more—even though the challenge of educating poorer children, many of whom are immigrants with poor English language skills or who have social or behavioral problems, is surely greater than the challenge of educating children from relatively more affluent households. De facto racial segregation has become the norm in schools in several large metropolitan areas.

Across the United States, public higher education is waning under severe budget constraints. Tuitions are rising faster than median family income. Meanwhile, elite colleges and universities are abandoning "need-blind" admissions policies, by which they guaranteed that any qualified student could afford to attend. Young people from families with incomes in the top 25 percent are three times more likely to go to college than are young people from the bottom quarter, and the disparity is increasing.

Why is the social contract coming undone—especially at the time when it's most needed? Part of the reason has to do with the same basic forces that have divided the workforce. Technological advances—primarily in information and communication—and global trade and investment have made a big portion of the tax base footloose. Capital can move at the speed of an electronic impulse. Well-educated professionals are also relatively mobile. They can move out of cities into remote suburbs where their property taxes don't have to pay for the costs of educating children poorer and needier than their own. They can work from home offices or office complexes in the country.

As a result of the mobility of capital and of the highly skilled, average and poorer working people find themselves bearing an increasingly large proportion of the cost of social programs—nationally, statewide, and in their own towns. Yet, as noted, the incomes of most people in the bottom half of the income ladder haven't risen along with the growth of the economy. Most are concerned with simply keeping their jobs.

Even this does not entirely explain the paradox. Today's wealthier investors and skilled professionals are not merely winners in a growing economy; they are also citizens in a splitting society. Why would they now allow the social contract to unravel? Are other forces weakening the bonds of affiliation and empathy on which a social contract is premised?

I do not have a clear answer, but I do have two hypotheses.

First, in the new global economy, those who are more skilled, more talented, or simply wealthier are not as economically dependent on the regional economy surrounding them as they once were, and thus have less self-interest in ensuring that their fellow inhabitants are as productive as possible. Alexis de Tocqueville noted in his book *Democracy in America* that the better-off Americans he met in his travels of the 1830s invested in their communities not out of European notions of honor, duty, and noblesse oblige, but because they knew they would reap some of the gains from the resulting economic growth. "The Americans are fond of explaining almost all the actions of their lives by the principle of self-interest rightly understood; they show with complacency how an enlightened regard for themselves constantly prompts them to assist one another and inclines them willingly to sacrifice a portion of their time and property to the welfare of the state." Today, increasingly, the geographic region within which a highly skilled individual lives is of less direct consequence to his or her economic well-being. It's now possible to be linked directly by modem and fax to the great financial or commercial centers of the world.

Second, any social contract is premised on "it could happen to me" thinking. Social insurance assumes that certain risks are commonly shared. Today's wealthy and poor, however, are likely to have markedly different life experiences. Disparities have grown so large that even though some of the rich (or their children) may become poor and some of the poor (or their children) will grow rich, the chances of either occurring are less than they were several decades ago. The wealthy are no longer under a "veil of ignorance" about their futures, to borrow philosopher John Rawls's felicitous phrase. They know that any social contract is likely to be one-sided; they and their children will be required to subsidize the poor and theirs.

Should you care? Yes. Even if the poorer members of our society were gaining a bit of ground while the richer were gaining far more, you might still have cause for concern. After a point, as inequality widened, the bonds that kept our society together would snap. Every decision we tried to arrive at together—about trade, immigration, education, taxes, and social insurance (health, welfare, retirement)—would be harder to make, because it would have such different consequences for the relatively rich than for the relatively poor. We could no longer draw upon a common reservoir of trust and agreed-upon norms to deal with such differences. We would begin to lose our capacity for democratic governance.

But even if you were willing to accept such dire consequences as the price for improving everyone's standard of living, you might not accept what's actually been happening. The economy has grown, inequality has widened, and the rich have grown richer while the poorer members of our society have been *losing* ground.

America as a whole is richer than it has been at any time in its history—richer than any other nation in the world—richer, by far, than any nation in the history of the world. And yet a significant portion of our population has become poorer over the last two decades. We have a new class of full-time worker. They're called the "working poor." Although they work at least forty hours a week, they don't earn enough to lift themselves and their families out of poverty. And behind the business cycle, the trend continues.

Global terrorism now poses the largest threat to our survival. But the widening split between our have-mores and have-lesses poses the largest threat to our strength as a society.

I don't want to depress you; I want to alarm you. America is overwhelmingly optimistic, practical, and innovative when it comes to solving big problems. But that's my point, really. Now's the time to tackle this widening gap—to reknit the social contract.

How? I offer a number of ideas in the pages to come.

Hey, Reich, you might say. You were in Washington. You were a cabinet member in the Clinton administration. Why didn't you and your friends fix this problem? Well, we did raise the minimum wage, implement the Family and Medical Leave Act, close sweatshops, get millions of Americans the skills they need for better jobs, and get the economy back on track. But we didn't get everything done by a long shot.

The truth is, nothing happens in government unless citizens demand that it happen. The real reknitting of the social fabric has to begin where the threads are—where you and I both are. That requires, at bottom, that you, and I, and millions like us get involved.

Many Americans have given up on politics. As their incomes have become more precarious, they've lost confidence that the "system" will or can work in their interest. That cynicism has generated a self-fulfilling prophecy. Politicians stop paying much attention to people who are politically apathetic—who aren't involved. And the political inattention seems to justify the cynicism. Meanwhile, big corporations and wealthy interests have experienced the opposite—a virtuous cycle in which campaign contributions have attracted the rapt attention of politicians, the attention has elicited even more money, and that money has given the powerful even greater influence.

Don't get me wrong. As individuals, many people on the

winning side of the divide are concerned about the new inequality. But as participants within institutions committed either to preserving the status quo or gaining further economic advantage for their constituents—large corporations, trade associations, and assorted special-interest lobbies— their concern is often laundered out of the politics they indirectly pursue. Reforming campaign-finance laws will help. But such reforms alone won't guarantee a vibrant democracy.

Ultimately, there's only one answer. You've got to get involved, personally. Get on the phones. Get on E-mail. Get out the vote. Mobilize your friends. Reach out. Build bridges across class and race. Persuade people to get involved who haven't been involved before. Convince good people to run for office. Maybe run yourself. And then keep organizing and mobilizing.

The only way to reknit the social fabric is one thread at a time. The only way to regrow democracy is from the grass roots.

CHAPTER TWO

Corporate Citizenship

Dear Bill Gates:

The Justice Department's antitrust case against Microsoft is only the first round. There will be more litigation, I promise you.

That's why I've hired a fleet of Washington lobbyists to persuade Congress that the government's lawsuit is misguided and launched a "grass roots" Internet campaign to get people to send messages to their representatives saying the same thing. I've sent money to Republican and Democratic campaign committees, which will use it to benefit candidates sympathetic toward Microsoft. I've even organized lobbying in state capitals to get the message out to state lawmakers.

You see, I'm a shareholder of Microsoft. Not a big one, mind you. You may not even know that I'm one of your bosses—but I am, because under the law Microsoft's first responsibility is to maximize the value of my shares.

So all the money Microsoft has been spending lobbying and politicking—in part, my money—has been spent on my behalf, just as if it were being invested in a new software product.

But I've got to tell you, Bill: I'm not happy about what you've been doing with my money. That's because I'm not just a Microsoft shareholder. I'm also a United States citizen, and I have goals other than maximizing the value of my stock. I think it's a good thing antitrust laws are enforced against powerful companies. I don't want to live in a country dominated by the interests of a few big companies, not even the ones I own.

In short, I don't want Microsoft to maximize the value of my shares at the expense of my values as a citizen. When I bought my tiny piece of the company, I wasn't saying, "Take my money and do whatever's politically necessary to give me a big return on it." I was only asking the company to do whatever was technologically and economically necessary to give me a big return.

Yes, I could sell my Microsoft shares and invest the money elsewhere, following the age-old American principle that if you don't like it, leave. But I'd rather not. I still have a lot of confidence in the company's ability to make innovative software. Besides, it's getting hard to find a high-technology company these days that's not pouring money into politics. High technology is becoming high-influence peddling.

More important, lobbying efforts like Microsoft's violate an implicit bargain that major corporations have with America. Big companies argue that they have no social responsibility to the public at large, and that their only duty is to their shareholders.

A corporation's responsibilities to the public, the argument goes, are better addressed in the legislative process than inside corporate boardrooms. Okay, then: this division of authority allows me to exercise my economic rights by investing in companies while exercising my political rights by voting in elections. I can instruct Microsoft to increase the value of my shares while also instructing my political representatives to pass laws to make sure that a giant corporation doesn't get too powerful and harm anything I believe in as a citizen.

Yet big companies are investing more and more in politics. When a company like Microsoft uses extra-ordinary economic clout to try to reduce the budget of the Justice Department's Antitrust Division, for example, it crosses that line.

Trying to shift government away from what citizens would like and toward what shareholders would profit from raises questions about the larger bargain America

*has made with every giant corporation. Microsoft may
not realize it, but its political tactics are making an
eloquent case that it and other corporate behemoths
should be either more directly accountable to the public
or busted up.*

*And I'm not just anybody making this point. I'm one
of Microsoft's owners.*

Sincerely yours,

*Robert Reich
Shareholder and Citizen*

Since the election of 2000, there's not much countervailing power in Washington. Big business is largely in control of the machinery of government. If corporate America understood its long-term interest, it would use this moment to establish in the public's mind the principle that business can be trusted. But it's doing the opposite, and the danger for American business as a whole is profound. After burying Washington in campaign contributions, Enron got exactly what it wanted: changes in regulations, loopholes in laws, and at least six audiences with White House officials during deliberations on the new national energy policy. All this allowed Enron to create a mammoth energy-finance company based, apparently, on blue smoke and opaque mirrors.

Enron isn't the only beneficiary. Credit-card companies

are getting a bankruptcy bill that will make it harder for over-stretched people who succumbed to these companies' blandishments ever to get out from under the resulting debts. Pharmaceutical companies are seeking longer patent protections. Big labor-intensive businesses want to get rules that weaken unions. They've already killed the Labor Department's ergonomics rule, which would have protected workers against repetitive-stress injuries.

In normal times—when business has to cope with some political resistance—its leaders are forced to set strict priorities. There is only a fixed amount of political capital to spend. The Business Roundtable, comprising the chief executives of the largest American companies, typically establishes at the start of a new Congress a legislative agenda reflecting what its members consider the most important issues. The United States Chamber of Commerce, after canvassing its mostly small and medium-size member businesses to determine their priorities, also develops a strategy. The National Association of Manufacturers weighs in with its wish list. And the National Federation of Independent Business, composed of small firms, sets its goals.

These groups do not always see eye to eye, but under normal circumstances they understand that legislative success requires coordination. Separately, they lack the political clout to overcome determined resistance in one or both houses of Congress or from a president at least partly dependent for his political future on organized labor, environmentalists, and other interests besides business.

The trade associations representing specific industries—coal-powered utilities, pharmaceuticals, hospitals, electronics, securities, oil and gas, for example—typically play supporting roles. Their own parochial legislative goals can't interfere directly with the priorities of business as a whole because the industries often have to depend on the larger business groups to be heard. Specific firms may retain their own Washington lobbyists, but they, too, have to work with others in order to have a significant effect.

Political resistance, in other words, usually forces the business community to decide what's most important to it. It thereby enables corporate America to exert some discipline over itself. Business leaders can prevent or at least distance themselves from excesses by any single company or industry that might otherwise taint business as a whole in the minds of the public.

American business notably did not come to the aid of cigarette manufacturers when lawsuits against them began several years ago. Nor has corporate America as a whole fought on behalf of the gun lobby. Labor and environmental rules with broad consequences typically become high priorities for legislative attack, but not all such rules. In the first Clinton administration, the business community was quite happy to let the Labor Department target apparel manufacturers and major retailers in its crackdown on sweatshops. I recall a number of White House meetings in which the leaders of major business organizations quietly assented to the administration's plans to block subsidies flowing to a particular industry, or to impose new clean-air rules on another industry, or to move aggressively with an antitrust complaint.

But with political resistance gone, the business community can no longer discipline itself. Every business lobbyist on K Street in Washington is under enormous pressure from clients to reap something from the new bonanza. Every trade association must demonstrate to its members large returns from their investments in getting a business-friendly government. And the pressure only ratchets upward: Every time one company or one industry receives its reward, other Washington lobbyists, representing other firms or industries, come under even more pressure to score victories.

Washington is awash in corporate IOUs, all waiting to be cashed in, and George W. Bush can't argue that the Democrats will block the payoffs. At this writing, Democrats barely control the Senate—and a few of those Democratic senators might as well be Republicans for the little resistance they show. Under these circumstances, the Bush forces are finding it difficult to maintain order.

In war-fevered Washington, politicians of all stripes are only too eager to accommodate proposed subsidies, loan guarantees, tax breaks, and regulatory relief for industries termed "vital" to the antiterrorist effort. The president says we need to be less dependent on foreign sources of oil, so we should allow American oil companies to drill on Alaska's coastal plain and also relax other environmental standards.

The airline bailout was notable not only for its size (its price tag exceeded the combined market value of United,

American, Delta, Northwest, US Airways, America West, and Continental), but also the speed and near unanimity with which it was granted. The sharp drop in business in the wake of September 11 surely imperiled airline balance sheets. But whatever might have happened to airline *companies,* America's aviation *system*—aircraft, telecom equipment, pilots, and crews—wasn't about to disappear. If some companies went bankrupt, other companies would buy their equipment and hire their employees. In the unlikely event that a significant percent of Americans never want to fly again, there's no reason why taxpayers should subsidize more of an aviation system than passengers need. And if the industry is going to shrink anyway, investors and consumers are better positioned to determine which airlines should survive than a government board doling out loan guarantees. Public funds could be put to better use helping airline employees find new jobs outside the industry, get retrained, and relocate themselves and their families.

Some proponents of subsidies or protections argue that America should have more capacity within its borders than the market demands, or risk not having enough oil, jet airplanes, or other "vital" assets during wartime. But how much domestic capacity? And what's vital? As a practical matter, we can better reduce the risk by not becoming too dependent on imports from any one country or region, stockpiling certain critical reserves, conserving our natural resources, and relying more on renewable sources of energy.

Even if we'd feel more secure with certain capacity inside the United States, subsidizing or protecting American-owned businesses is hardly the most efficient way to get it. American companies are developing capacity all over the world. During the week immediately after the attacks, even as United Airlines was warning Congress it faced imminent bankruptcy, its parent company was wiring $11.25 million to a French airplane manufacturer as a down payment on an order of thirty luxury business jets, each of which will cost about $20 million. The purchase is United's prerogative, of course. Its business is to maximize the value of its shares. But the transaction should at least raise the question of what public purpose Congress and the president thought they were achieving by bailing out the industry.

Meanwhile, a growing chorus is telling Americans that one of the best ways to demonstrate that the nation won't be cowed by terrorism is to continue to buy shares of stock and a lot of retail goods. Vice President Cheney said he hoped Americans would "stick their thumb in the eye of the terrorists and . . . not let what's happened here in any way throw off their normal level of economic activity." President Bush asked Americans for their "continued participation and confidence in the American economy."

Call it market patriotism.

The theory is that we demonstrate our resolve to the rest of the world by investing and consuming at least as much as we did before, preferably more. The terrorists tried to strike at the heart of American capitalism. We show that American capitalism is alive and well by using our credit cards as much as possible.

But spending seems like an odd way to demonstrate patriotism. Patriotism normally suggests a willingness to sacrifice for the good of the nation—if not lives, fortunes, and sacred honor, at least normal creature comforts. Market patriotism, on the other hand, suggests a strange kind of sacrifice: Continue the binge we've been on for years.

Usually, it's just the opposite in wartime. Consumers are asked to tame their appetites. And if voluntary restraints don't work, government resorts to rationing.

During World War II, each American was limited to half a pound of sugar a week, and each family to three gallons of gas and modest portions of meat, fuel oil, coffee, and cigarettes. Many consumer goods were simply unavailable. After 1942, you couldn't buy a new car because automakers had switched to making military vehicles. Silk stockings couldn't be found anywhere except perhaps on the black market. Even whiskey disappeared from shelves as distilleries converted to producing industrial alcohol. Meanwhile, consumers were solemnly instructed to save tin cans, scrap iron, paper, and tires. Millions of housewives even signed a Consumer's Victory Pledge: "As a consumer, in the total defense of democracy, I will . . . buy carefully. I will take good care of the things I have. I will waste nothing."

But now, in fighting terrorists, our patriotic duty seems to be to buy more and save less. The difference, of course, is that full-scale war mobilization requires a lot of the nation's productive capacity. The war effort comes first; consumer needs second. To make those priorities stick, consumer spending has to be constrained.

We're not in a full-scale war mobilization, and hopefully we won't be. In fact, right now America still has a lot of productive capacity that's not being used—which creates a problem of its own. The immediate economic threat isn't that we can't produce enough to meet demands. It's that there isn't enough demand for what we can produce. And since consumer spending accounts for two-thirds of all economic activity, any hesitancy on the part of consumers could spell big trouble—as it already has for the nation's airlines. The worry is that, having endured the horror of September 11, and fearing more to come, American consumers will pull in their belts another several notches.

Keeping consumers confident has been especially important since the start of the downturn in early 2001, because American consumers have almost single-handedly kept the U.S. economy afloat. Businesses stopped buying much of anything. They overspent in the late nineties, mostly on capital equipment and software, and began cutting back in 2000 at the first sign of trouble. The technology sector took the initial hit, but as profits continued to drop, capital investment of all kinds plummeted.

So American consumers have been about the only bright lights in the global-capitalist firmament. Yet the reality is that Americans are in no position to do what's being asked of them. Even before the terrorist attacks, personal savings rates were nearing a seventy-year low and personal debt was at record highs. Mortgage debt was in the stratosphere.

Despite the patriotic calls to invest in the stock market right now, the sad truth is that many middle-income Americans got into the market way over their heads during the boom years of the late nineties. Their spending binge after 1997 was fueled in part by the rapidly escalating value of their stock portfolios. They assumed they had fat nest eggs, only to discover this year that their nests contain tiny robin's eggs. And now they're worried about their paychecks.

Just before the terrorist attacks, the prudent thing for most families to do was to trim their budgets somewhat, pay down more of their debts, and put a bit more of their savings into bonds. After the terrorist attacks, that's still prudent behavior. There's no patriotism in being a spendthrift, no heroism in exposing one's family to unwarranted financial stress.

If political leaders want a display of market patriotism, an appropriate target would be profitable companies on the verge of announcing new rounds of mass layoffs. Companies should be asked to forbear laying off more workers, if they possibly can, for the duration of the war emergency. What better way of demonstrating we're all in this together?

Recall the first tenet of the social contract, which survived well into the 1970s. It assumed that companies had responsibilities beyond maximizing profits and bound companies to their workers and their communities. So long as a company earned healthy profits, employees could count on secure jobs with rising wages and benefits, and communities could count on a steady tax base. When the economy turned sour, employees might be laid off for a time. But when the economy revived, the work would return. The term "layoff" indicated a temporary separation.

Now that most corporations no longer feel responsibilities toward employees and communities, the contract has come undone. To put it very simply, as Hollywood movies evolved over forty years from George Bailey's Bedford Falls in *It's a Wonderful Life* to Gordon Gekko's *Wall Street*, the structure of the American economy was doing much the same thing.

What changed? Vast amounts of capital can now be moved from place to place at the push of a key on a personal computer. Investors face an ever-wider array of choices of where to put their money. The result is "electronic capitalism"—a worldwide system for immediately redeploying financial assets to where they can earn their highest return. Today, any chief executive who subordinates all else to maximize short-term profits can reap handsome rewards. Enron is "Exhibit A" in the rogues' gallery of corporate irresponsibility. Its motto seems to have been: We'll do whatever we can get away with to artificially boost our share price so top executives can loot the store.

Just at the time when the workforce is most in need of help adapting to a new economic system, the drastic narrowing of the sense of corporate mission has sharply limited the private sector's capacity to respond to that need.

As corporations have focused more and more exclusively

on increasing shareholders' immediate returns, pink slips have proliferated, health care and pensions have been cut, and the paychecks of most employees have gone nowhere. Employees without adequate education and skills, or with outmoded skills, are in free fall.

Do companies have obligations beyond the bottom line? Do they have a duty to their employees and their communities? Over the long term, do the interests of all stakeholders—shareholders, employees, and communities—begin to converge? And if they do, can we build a new social contract—a new corporate citizenship—on the basis of that convergence?

After all, Americans haven't abandoned their expectations of corporate citizenship. A 1996 poll sponsored by *Business Week* found that 95 percent of Americans believe that companies have responsibilities to their employees and their communities that go beyond making profits.

As I said at the start of this chapter, government must be free to stop companies from pursuing profits in ways that harm the public. Big companies that use their political muscle to prevent government from policing this line are, in effect, setting themselves up for much more intrusive forms of public vigilance. Enron is a case in point. But here's the good news—and it lies at the opposite extreme from Enron: There's growing evidence that good corporate citizenship enhances long-term profits.

Consider, for example, family-friendly workplaces. Businesses that help their workers fulfill their family responsibilities—policies such as flexible work schedules, help with child care, and generous leave for family and medical reasons—reduce costly turnover and retain valued employees. Many firms already offer these amenities to their high-paid creative workers in order to better attract and retain them, although few such benefits are available further down the hierarchy. The Family and Medical Leave Act requires employers to give their workers up to twelve weeks unpaid leave for the birth of a child or to care for an ailing relative. Some companies are proving that they can go beyond the minimum the law requires—and can boost the bottom line at the same time.

Evidence shows that these kinds of commitments pay for themselves in improved employee morale and productivity. Employees at Johnson & Johnson missed 50 percent less work after flexible work arrangements were instituted. A division of another major corporation found that flexible work schedules reduced absenteeism by 30 percent.

The second way companies can be good citizens is by providing their workers with health care and pension benefits. Here, too, government has a role to play in setting minimum standards. But with millions of American workers lacking both health care and pension coverage, it is clear that businesses must do more than meet the bare minimum—and it's clear that top-flight companies can, and do. Starbucks, for example, has been widely recognized for its practice of extending full health insurance benefits and its 401(k) plan to its *part-time* workers.

Thirdly, businesses should invest in their "human capital"—in upgrading the skills of their workers—which are so critical to raising incomes, increasing productivity, and growing the economy.

One study has found that companies that introduced formal employee training programs experienced a 19 percent larger rise in productivity than firms that did not train their workers. Another shows that raising the average education of a workforce by one year helps them become as much as 12 percent more productive.

Some companies have received that message loud and clear. Granite Rock, a construction materials supplier in Watsonville, California, invests more than $2,000 per employee annually in training—nearly thirteen times the industry average. Workers at Cin-Made, an Ohio firm that makes specialized packaging, receive extensive on-the-job training and additional pay for acquiring advanced skills. And Harley-Davidson, maker of the legendary motorcycles, has established an on-site learning center for its employees.

These investments in skills have paid off for each of these companies. Granite Rock has improved customer service and raised its productivity to 30 percent above the industry average. Cin-Made has seen its on-time deliveries increase by nearly a third. And, after some tough years, Harley-Davidson is back on top of the motorcycle market.

The fourth thing businesses can do is to work in partnership with their employees—giving them a greater voice in the enterprise and sharing the benefits of the good years, not just the burdens of the bad.

Consider this: A study by the Wyatt Company, a business management consultant firm, of 531 mostly large companies found that although three quarters of the companies had cut their payrolls in the economic downturn of the early nineties, most reported that the cuts had failed to achieve their expected results. Of the companies surveyed, earnings increased just for 46 percent of them; while 58 percent expected higher productivity, only 34 experienced it; while 61 percent sought to improve customer service, only 33 percent concluded that they'd achieved it.

And in another study, MIT researchers compared two groups of automobile factories that were similar in every respect except that in the first set, three practices—employee involvement, profit-sharing, and productivity gain-sharing —were followed; in the second, none. The study found that workers in the first set of factories manufactured vehicles eight hours faster, on average, than workers in the second, and with fewer defects per car.

Businesses can do a great deal more to reward their employees for abiding loyalty, dedication, and hard work—as many companies already have. Intel, for example, is known far and wide for its strong fringe benefits, deferred profit-sharing plan, and commitment to redeploying workers instead of laying them off.

After a fire destroyed Malden Mills in Lawrence, Massachusetts, in the mid-nineties, its owner, Aaron Feuerstein, could have given his workers pink slips and run off with a fat check from the insurance company. But Feuerstein rebuilt the factory and continued to pay his workers in the meantime. Malden Mills is still struggling, but its most valuable asset is its loyal and dedicated employees.

Here's a final example, also from the great state of Massachusetts: Rather than resort to massive layoffs when profits fell off a cliff in 2001, Axcelis Technologies kept most of its people employed—using vacation days, volunteer furloughs, temporary shutdowns, and cuts in travel and nonessential items. At the depths of the recession, in February 2002, it even opened a new 140,000-square-foot semiconductor manufacturing demonstration facility. "Keeping people employed and continuing to invest will pay big dividends when the recession is over," Mary Puma, Axcelis's CEO, told me.

Perhaps the most telling stories of the year came out of New York. With massive layoffs throughout the city in the wake of the terrorist attacks, Eric Villency, president of the furniture chain Maurice Villency, pledged to retain all two hundred of his employees even though profits were down 10 percent. Southwest Airlines and Saturn Corporation also vowed to retain workers, even though their competitors in both airline and car industries have slashed payrolls. My betting is that these companies will do even better than before, because their employees will be willing to go the extra mile for them.

The experience of many companies shows that allowing workers to share the gain as well as the pain, and giving them a genuine voice in the enterprise, is a successful strategy that pays big dividends over the long term. At times layoffs may be necessary, of course, but companies that treat their workers as assets to be developed rather than as costs to be cut use layoffs only as a last resort, and only after giving their employees every opportunity to find new, productive work.

Finally, responsible businesses can build partnerships with public schools in a coordinated strategy to help students most at risk in the new economy. Instead of starving public schools in communities where firms are headquartered—by demanding tax breaks from the community as a condition for coming and staying—businesses can collaborate with public schools to design and staff "apprenticeships" for jobs that would await students after graduation. Too often, high school students not bound for college are dumped into old-fashioned vocational-education classes that are little more than holding bins, irrelevant to real-world jobs. What students most need is technical training by skilled employees, within apprenticeship programs carefully designed to supplement classroom work.

Some cynics say that business leaders can't be expected to care about the economic fate of their fellow Americans. They see Enron as an emblem for all of corporate America. I just don't believe that. The idea that bad citizenship makes good business sense would be seen as bizarre by most Americans, including most business leaders, throughout most of our country's history. Everybody remembers GM's "Engine Charlie" Wilson's creed that "what's good for General Motors is good for America." But we often forget the second part of that declaration—"And vice versa." The common interest of corporation and culture was a matter of simple common sense to most business people, until recently. And I'm confident that we'll soon dismiss the extreme notion that business can prosper while the middle class withers and the civic culture decays. We'll return to the older view that corporations are, in a sense, citizens of our American community, that citizenship carried duties as well as rights, and that there is and must be an ethical basis to doing business in America.

It is already apparent that the vast majority of Americans—including many of our nation's business leaders—still believe that there should be a social contract. A number of companies are doing the right thing today. Over the long term, doing right is consistent with doing well. As a society—as consumers, investors, and citizens—we should encourage other companies to follow their lead.

I learned about the power of consumers when I was Secretary of Labor. After we discovered sweatshops in the garment industry—crowded, unsanitary cutting and sewing shops that weren't even paying minimum wages—we announced the names of the major-brand manufacturers and big retailers that had contracted with them. As a result, consumers put enormous pressure on these well-known manufacturers and retailers. This in turn forced them to do a better job monitoring their contractors and subcontractors. Companies that could assure consumers their garments weren't made in sweatshops gained a competitive advantage. Sweatshops haven't been eradicated completely, but consumer pressure has had a big impact.

Look, I'm not so naive as to believe that all companies will realize that acting responsibly toward their employees and communities is good for their long-term bottom lines. Many CEOs—and many investors—don't think beyond the next quarter. Not all companies understand the benefits of social responsibility. So we can't let them capture government. Government must be vigilant in protecting the interests of employees, investors, and communities. But perhaps we can look forward to more collaboration between government and business that enhances rather than guts responsibility.

The good news is that some companies are catching on. Consumers and investors are starting to look closely at how companies behave. "Socially responsible" investing is becoming popular. The Enron scandal itself has produced something of a backlash against corporate irresponsibility. Even campaign-finance reform is getting a second wind.

In short, we may be on the verge of a new understanding of corporate citizenship—that's really a return to a very old, very basic American norm.

CHAPTER THREE

Work That Pays, Insurance if It Doesn't

It's been said that in Washington a "gaffe" occurs when a high-level official accidentally says what he means. The Bush administration has been remarkably gaffe-free so far, with almost everyone sticking to the same bland script. All except Treasury Secretary Paul O'Neill, that is, whose gaffes offer a glimpse into the real philosophy of the administration that now runs the United States. O'Neill's latest occurred in an interview with the *Financial Times* in which he questioned why the government should provide Social Security, Medicare, or any other social insurance. "Able-bodied adults should save enough on a regular basis so that they can provide for their own retirement and, for that matter, health and medical needs," he said.

The Treasury secretary raises one of the most fundamental questions society faces: Why should there be any social insurance at all?

The idea for Social Security was dreamed up by Labor Secretary Frances Perkins and signed into law by Franklin D. Roosevelt in 1935. Unemployment insurance and welfare were parts of the original scheme. Medicare was President Johnson's doing, thirty years later.

The broad idea was easily understood by the generations

that experienced the Depression, World War II, the Cold War, and some deep recessions. Any family could find itself down on its luck through no fault of its own. Family savings could go down the drain if the economy turned really sour. Its breadwinner might lose his (almost always "his") job and have a hard time finding another. Or he might become disabled or die, leaving his wife and children destitute. An elderly person or couple might lose everything in an economic downdraft and face their twilight years in grinding poverty.

A decent society, it was assumed, would pool some of its resources to guard against these personal misfortunes. Like any insurance system, citizens would be expected to pay premiums. But unlike private insurance, everyone would be included regardless of the likelihood they'd need to draw on the insurance pool. Rich and poor, healthy and sick, young workers and older workers—all would pitch in.

Treasury Secretary O'Neill would prefer going back to the days before social insurance, when individuals either had to save their own earnings against the possibility they'd need help down the line or buy their own private insurance. Presumably, if the responsibility rested entirely on their shoulders, they'd save more and take better precautions to avoid harm's way.

Some families, however, don't earn enough to allow them to save much of anything. And some harms—a catastrophic illness, a disabling accident, a factory closing, a stock-market plunge—can't be avoided.

Meanwhile, private insurers naturally will do everything they can to sign up clients at the lowest risk of needing them, while avoiding the high risks. After all, insurance companies and HMOs aren't charitable institutions. They need to show profits. And all are becoming more efficient at discriminating among potential consumers, weeding out the high risks and marketing to the low.

So without social insurance, people who are poorer or who face higher risk of having bad things happen to them won't be covered. People at the other end—richer and at lower risk—will efficiently pool their resources and get insurance at a much lower rate than if they had to bear the extra cost of insuring the poorer and riskier.

It's coming to be like that all over the land. The richer, healthier, younger, well-educated, and well-connected and their children are doing better and better. (They even get a big tax windfall now.) And the gap between them and the bottom half of the nation widens.

Secretary O'Neill's vision is on its way to becoming reality. Much of the "safety net" provided by the Social Security Act of 1935 is already in shreds. And now Social Security and Medicare are on the dock. The administration wants to "privatize" them by letting the younger, healthier, and richer opt out.

In America work is a citizen's most fundamental economic responsibility. It is the essence of the Protestant ethic, the criterion for being considered a "deserving" member of society. Once this responsibility is fulfilled, the burden of ensuring a healthy economy shifts back to society.

In this light, the implicit moral code that has undergirded

working life is revealed for what it is—neither the outcome of political deals nor a set of crass intrusions into the free market, but simple ethical norms that affirm human dignity: Anyone who's willing and able to work hard should be able to get ahead. His or her family shouldn't live in poverty. Everyone should be able to make the most of their talents and abilities.

Why else would 80 percent of the American public in poll after poll strongly favor an increase in the minimum wage? After all, it benefits only a small and politically impotent fraction of the workforce.

Why the storm of public outrage when we discovered that the Kathie Lee line of clothing was made, in part, in a Manhattan sweatshop where workers were paid a small fraction of the minimum wage? Most of those workers don't even speak English.

And why, by contrast, did the public make such a hero of Aaron Feuerstein, the president of Malden Mills, who promised his blue-collar workers continued employment when his mill burned down just before Christmas in 1995. After all, blue-collar workers have been taking it on the chin for years.

These sentiments seem to defy what we've come to assume about these parched times—that people are concerned only about their own advancement, that our public conversation reflects no more than a series of contests between interest groups competing for special advantage, and that, when it comes to the economy, workers should be paid no more than what the market says they're worth.

Work has always been more than just an economic transaction. It helps define who we are. It confirms our usefulness. What we do on the job—the people with whom we work, and the ways in which our bosses, our colleagues, our customers, patients, clients, or charges respond to our work—gives meaning and dignity to our lives.

Dignity at work is not simply a matter of status or power. Someone who empties bedpans can feel as worthy as one who controls billions of dollars of investments. Dignity depends in a large part, I think, on whether one feels valued. And the sense of being valued at work comes both from appreciation shown by others, and from one's own pride in doing a job well, no matter how humble. In this respect, work is a moral act as well as an economic one.

This moral reality is often obscured, but has come into sharper focus for the middle class as jobs have grown more precarious. The omnipresent threat that an employer may at any time contract the same work to someone else who will do it more cheaply, or cosign it to a machine capable of doing it more efficiently, has had a profound effect.

It's not just that paychecks have become less stable and living standards less secure. That's true, of course, and poses the largest and most immediate problem. But this precariousness also has made millions of middle- and lower-income people feel less valued. Whatever meaning and dignity they once derived from work has been diminished by this new humbling sense of easy expendability.

Many people I meet around the country express sadness

about the evanescence of their jobs. They don't necessarily blame their employers; many even sympathize. But even those who aren't particularly worried about finding a new job are hurt by how little it appears to matter how well they do their current one.

Perhaps it is this subtle humiliation that is beginning to sensitize many middle-class Americans to the vulnerabilities of other working people. Not only is the possibility of downward mobility more palpable, but the threat to self-respect is more immediate. The cultural gap that used to separate middle-income workers from the working poor or those in need of state assistance seems somewhat narrower.

Some politicians have celebrated the decline in America's welfare rolls without acknowledging that millions of people who are now at work but had been on welfare are not earning enough to support their families. They are in dead-end jobs without a future. Yet a positive political consequence of welfare reform has been to move several million people from being considered "undeserving poor" because they don't work to being viewed as "deserving" poor because they do. Most former welfare recipients are as poor as they were before, but the fact that they now work for their meager living has altered the politics surrounding the question of what to do about their poverty.

Welfare became deeply unpopular in America when the loss of manufacturing jobs required many women to work in order to maintain family incomes that previously had been sustained by one male worker. Many of these working women were mothers of young children. These families saw no reason why women who were only slightly poorer than they should be able to stay home with their children and receive welfare benefits.

But now that all struggling Americans are more or less in the same sinking boat, there's less reason for working families to resent the poor. It's now possible to argue convincingly that all people on the bottom half of the income ladder should have access to better education and training, health care, and child care if they're going to be able to get ahead. And that work should pay enough for anyone to get by.

When I came to Washington at the start of 1993, many Democrats didn't want to talk about raising the minimum wage because it was seen as something that "old" Democrats worried about. Its real monetary value had eroded for years, and the poor workers who directly benefited from it were politically inactive. Yet as welfare reform came closer to becoming a political certainty, the moral argument for a higher minimum wage gained credence. How could America in good conscience expect millions of welfare recipients to work for a living if they couldn't earn enough to live on?

A sensible approach now would be to raise the minimum wage to its historic level—roughly half the median wage. That would put it at about seven dollars an hour. Thereafter index it to inflation. When combined with the Earned Income Tax Credit (EITC) and with food stamps, this higher minimum wage would lift a family with one full-time worker and two children out of poverty.

But there are limits. Raise the minimum wage too high and you might deter employers from hiring many low-skilled workers; the employers would sooner substitute automated machinery or not have the work done at all. Expand the EITC too much and you might deter employers from paying their workers adequately, knowing that taxpayers would make up the difference. We don't know exactly how high the minimum wage could be raised or how far the EITC could be expanded without causing these undesirable results, so there's room to experiment.

Unionization would also help. Although it's difficult to unionize low-wage workers—they tend to work in small establishments and are easily intimidated by employers who don't want unions—the fact that most low-wage workers are in the local service economy means their jobs won't drift abroad if employers have to pay more for them. And recent successes in unionizing health-care workers in California and in conducting a national campaign to lift the wages of janitors suggest larger possibilities ahead. But as with the minimum wage, there's a limit to how high unionized wages can go before employers find it cheaper to automate the jobs, cut back on staffing, or not offer the services to begin with.

Another means of raising wages: If the Federal Reserve Board allowed the economy to grow so fast that demand for low-wage workers exceeded the supply, their wages would rise. This is what happened between 1996 and 2000. Of course, this strategy could take us only so far before igniting inflation.

Ultimately, the best way to make work pay is to ensure that everyone has an education sufficient to raise their productivity and thereby warrant higher pay. This is a good and noble goal, worth pursuing, even if the beneficial results are years away.

Separately, none of these measures is sufficient. Together, a somewhat higher minimum wage, a somewhat expanded EITC, more unionization of low-wage workers, faster growth, and better education can lift full-time working families out of poverty. We don't know the ideal combination of these measures but the nation is surely rich enough and clever enough to try until we get it right.

Here's a final idea for helping the bottom half share in the nation's prosperity. Give them, literally, a share in America. Spread capitalism by spreading capital. Rather than just redistribute income to people after they've become poor, give them capital up front to build their fortunes. Give a young family a starter nest egg. Give a young adult a capital stake.

In the last few years, there have been several proposals for accomplishing this ambitious idea. One was President Clinton's proposed Universal Savings Accounts. The plan was introduced as part of Social Security reform. But it wasn't really about Social Security. It was about redistributing capital assets to lower-income families.

Here's how it would work. Families earning under $40,000 would get an annual $600 tax credit, plus another $700 if they deposited $700 of their own money into their account. This adds up to an annual nest egg of $2,000. If they continue saving in this way for forty years, assuming a modest 5 percent rate of return, their nest egg would accumulate into a brontosaurus egg of over $250,000. Higher-income families would get a smaller subsidy. Total cost to taxpayers: about $30 billion a year, most of which would go to poorer families.

Or consider former Senator Bob Kerrey's "Kid Save" plan. Here, the government would give every newborn a $1,000 savings account, to which $500 would be added every year until the child's fifth birthday. The money accumulates and the interest compounds until the child reaches twenty-one, and—presto!—the child has a cool $20,000 to start his or her adult life. The tab: about $15 billion a year.

There are other variations, but you get the point. Instead of redistributing income, redistribute capital. Encourage people to save and depend on their personal choices about how to invest money. This way we get the efficiency benefits of a market economy and also the social benefits of a more egalitarian society. It's a twofer.

Actually, the idea of up-front capital isn't as novel as it may seem. After all, the Homestead Act of 1862 gave 160 acres of Western land to anyone willing to settle there for five years. Much more recently, Margaret Thatcher invited residents of Britain's publicly owned housing (then almost a third of the country's housing stock) to purchase their homes at bargain-basement rates. And Czech prime minister Vaclav Klaus auctioned off shares of state-owned companies to Czech citizens holding redeemable vouchers.

So why the interest now? Three reasons.

First, it's dawning on many people that the old ways of trying to broaden prosperity aren't working nearly as well or as fast as we'd like. As I've noted, the median American family is, in real economic terms, not much better off today than it was a decade ago, even though its members are working longer hours—the equivalent of seven more weeks a year— than they did then.

Meanwhile, it's become clear that we can't rely on direct handouts and income transfers to do the job. They have all sorts of negative side effects, such as dependency. And there's no political will to carry them out on a large scale. Trying to redistribute income from rich to poor through specific federal programs financed by annual appropriations, including everything from Head Start to low-income housing, has become particularly difficult.

The second reason for the new conversation is that capital assets—rather than income—are now where the action is. The story of the 1990s, if you hadn't noticed, was the extraordinary boom in the market valuations of companies, followed by homes, and even American dollars. Yes, I know, the stock-market boom ended with a thud. But even so, stock prices are still about three times higher today than they were at the start of the 1990s—which is more than can be said for incomes.

Most Americans haven't got much out of this capital boom, however, because most don't have much capital. While almost half of American families own some shares of stock nowadays, most of those holdings are valued under $5,000. Young families are even less likely to own capital. The average young family has a net worth of only about $12,000, including the value of the family car. Fewer than half own a home, which is usually heavily mortgaged. The typical young family in the bottom half of the earnings ladder has a net worth of $2,000, or less.

The biggest single consequence of the nineties bull market was to make those who were already rich before 1991 fabulously richer. The wealthiest 10 percent of Americans received 85 percent of Wall Street's gains. The wealthiest 1 percent got 40 percent of them.

Even with the stock market sagging, the wealth gap endures. When the parents of today's baby boomers leave this world, the wealthier of them will also leave behind a collection of assets worth hundreds of billions of dollars more than they paid for them. Their boomer offspring will inherit the largest intergenerational windfall in the history of modern civilization. And thanks to the "stepped-up-basis-at-death" tax rule, these assets will arrive free of capital-gains taxes.

The tax favors don't end there. Those who have earned enough to be able to invest in this buoyant capital market are also advantaged by rules allowing them to defer income taxes on that portion of their incomes. The resulting benefits are wildly tilted toward the very people who are already gaining the most from the surge in capital values. Two-thirds of all the tax benefits for pensions and retirement savings now go to families earning more than $100,000 a year. Only 7 percent of these benefits go to families earnings $50,000 or less.

The asset elevator has been lifting America's wealthy to

ever-higher vistas, without their moving a muscle (except, perhaps, to speed-dial their brokers). Current tax law is lifting them, and their children, even higher. Hence the case for allowing the rest of America on the elevator, too. Whether it's government-subsidized "universal savings accounts" for Americans of modest means, or schemes to give every young adult a certain amount of capital, the goal is the same—to let everyone in on the ride.

It's no substitute for social insurance, and no replacement for other ways to make work pay. But redistributing capital, and encouraging saving, is an important means of widening the circle of prosperity. Maybe even Treasury Secretary O'Neill could get behind this one.

CHAPTER FOUR

Lifelong Learning: Education for the Twenty-first Century

The third promise of the American social contract: Everyone should be able to get ahead by making full use of his or her talents and abilities. Here again, there's broad agreement, and has been for a long time. This was the basic argument underlying the free-school movement of the nineteenth century, the high school movement of the early twentieth, and the vast expansion of public universities after World War II. It should now be the basic argument for ensuring that an excellent system of education and job training be available to all Americans, not just the better-off. And that all families can afford child care that keeps preschoolers safe and stimulates their rapidly developing minds.

Education isn't just a nice thing to do to the extent we can afford it. It's the single most important public investment in our future. Lifelong learning—beginning in early childhood and extending all the way through a person's career—has to become the norm for all our people. The thing about the twenty-first-century economy that distinguishes it most sharply from the economy that preceded it is the central importance of people's minds, and skills. "Human capital" is the asset that matters most.

Evidence is mounting that very young children—infants,

toddlers, preschoolers—need attention and stimulation if they're to thrive later in life. The National Research Council and Institute of Medicine's new report, "From Neurons to Neighborhoods: The Science of Early Childhood Development," shows that how children are treated in these early years is as important as what they're taught. Children who receive consistent and attentive care are better able to learn by the time they reach school age; those who don't receive it are left behind before they even start.

But many working families can't afford high-quality child care. Since most parents work, it's not surprising that over 60 percent of children under age four are in some sort of childcare arrangement during the day, including 44 percent of infants under a year. The cost ranges from around $4,000 a year per child to $20,000, but the low end is fundamentally different from the high.

Low-end care may provide a safe environment but has fewer caregivers per child than at the higher end, the caregivers have less training, and they are more likely to leave for another job in a short time. For these reasons, children in low-end care have less opportunity to form relationships with their caregivers than to children in high-end care. These differences in the amount, quality, and consistency of care can have significant consequences for children later in their lives.

A decent society in which most parents work would provide children with safe and stimulating child care. Childhood education would begin much earlier than kindergarten. And the school day for all children would extend until parents returned from work.

By far the biggest obstacle to upward mobility in this prosperous nation is the lousy schools so many poorer kids attend. There are two main reasons.

First, there's not nearly enough money. As I've noted, about half of school revenues come from local property taxes. Increasingly, though, Americans are segregating by income in terms of where they choose to live. Entire towns are now either rich, poor, blue collar, or middle class. That means poorer districts have lower tax bases, which translates into fewer dollars per pupil. Court-ordered state "equalization formulas" seeking to redress the financial imbalance haven't worked. An analysis from the National Center for Education Statistics shows that most poor students live in districts that spend less per student than their state's average. One in four poor kids receives between 10 and 30 percent less than students from middle-income families.

It shouldn't be surprising, then, that poorer schools are more run-down than schools in richer communities, that they have fewer new books, and that their equipment is more outmoded. Their teachers don't earn as much as teachers in richer schools, even though the challenges they face are more formidable. No wonder that, as the U.S. Department of Education recently reported, much of the teaching in schools serving poor communities is now done by teacher's aides without college degrees, instead of by qualified teachers.

The second reason poor kids attend lousy schools is that most of the other kids who attend them are also poor. Poverty in America is becoming more geographically concentrated. So the poverty-related problems of these children—drugs, violence, unruly behavior, low self-esteem, and parents often too overwhelmed or overworked to give their children the attention they need—are compounded by the presence of many other kids with the same problems.

Peer effects among school-age children are significant— as any parent of a teenager will attest. High school students are less likely to go to college when fewer of their classmates are college-bound; more likely to get into trouble with the law when more of their classmates get into trouble; more likely to have babies out of wedlock when more of their peers are having babies. New evidence strongly suggests that peer effects extend beyond schools to the communities surrounding them. After a random sample of poor inner-city families in Boston received housing vouchers that enabled them to move to higher-income suburbs, their children's behavior improved relative to children in families who wanted the vouchers but lost out in the lottery.

Any sane approach to giving poor kids a better education would have to respond to both these reasons for why they're trapped in lousy schools. Instead of giving poor kids less money per pupil than middle-income kids get, give them more. Per-pupil public school expenditures now average

$6,000 to 7,000 a year in the United States (state averages range from $4,000 to $9,000). So back up every child from America's poorest 20 percent of families with $10,000 to $12,000, and children from families in the next quintile with $8,000 to $10,000.

At the same time, bust up the concentrations of poor kids in the same schools. Create incentives for them to disperse. Let any public school that meets strict standards of accountability compete to enroll these kids and receive the money that goes with them. That way, public schools in nearby wealthy suburban communities also will try to lure some of the poor kids their way in order to meet their budgets—perhaps sending out vans to collect them and drop them off.

Notice I haven't used the term "voucher." It's become so loaded—like abortion and communism—that you can't talk about vouchers without being tarred as either "for" or "against." Nothing else gets through. In a piece I wrote for the *Wall Street Journal*, I made a case for "progressive vouchers" and immediately became the liberal poster child for the pro-voucher movement. It was ironic because the whole point of the piece was that vouchers won't work. They'll just sort American children even more—further concentrating the kids who are more needy or troublesome, or whose parents are less able to cope, in schools that are even worse than before—as every slightly better-off child runs for the exits. Such schools would end up with even fewer resources per difficult child. America would become even more socially stratified. Let there be no mistake: Vouchers without a lot of extra money behind poorer kids are worse than no vouchers at all. We must not drain resources from our public schools, already resource poor. Poorer kids need more resources, not fewer.

So don't call my proposal a voucher scheme. Call it anything else. Call it liverwurst. My liverwurst scheme is designed to get more money to poor kids and break up concentrations of poor kids in the same institutions—in other words, to go after the core reasons that poor kids are locked in bad schools. This will be a hard sell, to say the least. Any hope for it requires a coalition of conservatives who want to give poor kids more choice and liberals who want to give them more money. But liverwurst is an idea whose time has come.

More dollars and more choice among public schools will help. But beware of another idea that's rapidly becoming an obsession: high-stakes standardized tests. They're the single biggest thing to have hit American education since *Sputnik*. Responding to the understandable demands for more "accountability," almost every school in the land is morphing into a test-taking factory.

There are obvious benefits. Uniform tests present clear goals and give students, parents, and schools ways to measure progress toward meeting them. But standardized tests are monstrously unfair to many kids. We're creating a one-size-fits-all system that needlessly brands many young people as failures, when they might thrive if offered a different education whose progress was measured differently.

I'm all in favor of making schools more accountable for what they do (or fail to do). By all means let's find out whether schools are doing their job by testing a random sample of kids in the school every year. Publish the test results without naming the kids. This would light a fire under schools that failed to make progress (unless, of course, so many children move in and out of the school every year that even these tests don't prove much about whether the school is doing better).

It's perfectly fine to test kids on whether they understand what they've learned in specific courses. When I was in public school I sweated through the New York State Regents exams, subject after subject. They did me no harm—maybe even some good.

But it seems grossly unfair to rely on one big, high-stakes exam to decide whether a child gets promoted to the next grade, and especially unfair to rely on one test to determine whether a kid graduates from high school.

Paradoxically, we're embracing high-stakes standardized tests just when the new economy is eliminating standardized jobs. There's one certainty about what today's high school students will be doing a decade from now: They won't all be doing the same things, and they won't all be drawing on the same body of knowledge.

Jobs in the old mass-production economy came in a few standard varieties (research, production, sales, clerical, managerial, professional), but this system has fragmented. Computers, the Internet, and digital commerce have exploded the old job categories into a vast array of new niches, creating a kaleidoscope of ways to make a living.

Musicians, artists, writers, and performing artists are discovering multimedia outlets for their talents. Tens of thousands of people are starting their own Web-based businesses and auction houses. People who had been clerks and secretaries are turning into spreadsheet operators, desktop publishers, and Web-based inventory control managers. Salespeople are becoming specialty technicians, finding or creating products to meet particular customer needs.

The Bureau of Labor Statistics projects that between 1990 and 2005 there will have been a 37 percent increase in the demand for "technicians." This job classification defies the traditional color scheme of the old economy, in which white-collar managers supervised blue-collar employees. Technicians often wear suits or ties (like white-collar types), but they also often work with their hands and use tools (like blue-collar types). They blur the old categories.

Technicians operate computers monitoring robots that assemble electronic equipment. They run tests on breakthrough drugs in the laboratories of biotechnology companies. They drive trucks equipped with modems and make just-in-time deliveries. They assist lawyers by going on-line to research cases and statutes. They manage sections of retail stores, periodically tapping PCs to determine which items are selling well and which may need a price cut. They install office machines and link them together in complex communications networks.

We're also seeing an increasing demand for people who provide personal attention and comfort. There's an upsurge in advisers, counselors, coaches, and trainers. Physical and occupational therapists are needed. Home health-care workers, elder-care assistants and child-care workers are all in short supply. And we have a chronic need for teachers at all levels.

Success in these jobs doesn't depend on mastery of one uniform body of knowledge as measured by a single high-stakes standardized test. Instead, these new careers require an ability to learn on the job—to discover what needs to be known and to find and use it quickly. Some depend on creativity—on out-of-the-box thinking, originality, and flair. Others depend on the ability to listen and understand what other people are feeling and needing. Most require "soft skills" like punctuality and courtesy (although some geeks succeed wildly without even these rudiments).

Yes, everyone needs to be able to read, write, and speak clearly. And they have to know how to add, subtract, multiply, and divide. But given the widening array of possibilities, there's no reason every child must master every aspect of algebra, geometry, biology, English, history, or any of the rest of the standard high school curriculum that has barely changed in half a century.

Nor does every high school graduate have to qualify for a liberal arts college. The new jobs of our new economy typically require some education beyond high school but not necessarily a four-year college degree.

In our headlong rush toward "accountability," we seem to be veering toward two extremes—either expecting every child to pass the same test or assuming that certain children have limited intellectual capacity and must be relegated to an old-fashioned vocational track. Yet in the new economy, traditional vocational skills soon become obsolete. Besides, the whole notion of faster or slower learning is irrelevant when there are so many new options for how and what to learn.

The best way to increase the wages of most Americans is to equip all Americans to earn their own prosperity. The evidence is overwhelming that the sharper a person's skills, the higher that person's wages. Each year of education or job training after high school, whenever it occurs in the course of a career, increases average incomes by 6 to 12 percent. Many technical skills can be learned in a year or two by someone with a high school degree. In fact, one goal we should consider is universal, high-quality K through 14. You heard me right: K through 14.

In the early twentieth century, states pioneered the concept of universal K through 12. The twentieth-century economy and society needed it. For most of the century, education beyond twelfth grade was a luxury. In the twenty-first century most young people also need at least two years of critical skills beyond the typical high school curriculum—technical skills, thinking skills, on-the-job learning skills.

By the same token, any young person who qualifies should be able to get a four-year college education. Yet for many young people and their families, this dream is becoming unaffordable.

Not long ago, the president of a prestigious university (not the one in which I now teach) was explaining his strategy to me. "We're very selective, but we need to become even more selective," he said. "Our SATs are rising, but not as fast as I'd like. We should be on par with . . ." and he named several institutions even more selective than the one he led. "We're going to market ourselves more intensively to high school stars," he told me.

I asked him about his new capital campaign and how much of the money raised would go to awarding scholarships to needy students or expanding the size of the entering class. Apparently, none. "We're going to build a new student center, upgrade the dorms, and use the rest to attract some faculty and student stars," he answered. "That's what our competitors are doing. We can't afford not to."

I nodded sympathetically. Still, it struck me that, if most college presidents were thinking the same way, the competition for the best and brightest (measured in conventional ways) was going to become more heated than it already is, and a lot of children from lower-income families weren't going to stand a chance.

Meanwhile, children from middle- and upper-income families continue to apply to four-year colleges in ever-greater numbers, and competition for admission to the most selective and prestigious institutions is rising steeply. Acceptance rates at the most selective institutions are dropping, even though high school guidance counselors have been trying to make students more realistic about their chances. For example, according to data published in a popular guide to colleges, in 1980 Harvard accepted 16 percent of its applicants; the most recent data, from 1998, show Harvard accepting 12 percent. Parents and students are similarly finding out that Stanford accepts only 13 percent of its applicants these days; twenty years ago, it accepted 19 percent. The pattern has been much the same at prestigious state universities like the University of Michigan at Ann Arbor, where the rate of acceptance dropped from 72 percent to 59 percent over the same interval.

With colleges seeking to be more selective, and more students seeking admission to the most selective, it's no surprise that the pressure on students and their families is rising. Even sixth graders are feeling it, according to a front-page story in the *New York Times*. The father of one eleven-year-old introduced the boy to a university admissions officer, who advised him to take Spanish rather than Latin and to sign up for calculus as soon as possible. Other sixth graders are surfing college home pages on the Web, eyeing future majors and financial-aid opportunities.

That such competitive pressures are building, among both colleges and their prospective students, seems an accepted aspect of contemporary American life. Yet, in my view, inadequate attention is being paid to the larger social consequences of the trend—especially to how higher-education resources are being allocated in this era of widening inequality.

Two broad forces are behind the headlong rush toward greater selectivity. The most basic is that the economic stakes of getting a degree from a reputable four-year college or university have become much higher, as disparities in income and wealth have widened nationwide.

By the end of the 1990s, according to data contained in the Census Bureau's annual Current Population Survey, the income gap between the top and bottom 10 percent of earners was wider than at any time since the 1920s. The richest 1 percent of American families, comprising 2.7 million people, had just about as many dollars to spend, after they had paid all taxes, as the bottom 100 million. And they owned most of America's marketable assets. That represents the largest concentration of both income and wealth in more than a century.

The purpose of college shouldn't be solely about earning a good income after graduation, of course, but the growing correlation between the amount of education and the level of earnings is striking. In 1998, according to the Census Bureau, the average income of families headed by someone with no more than a high school diploma was $48,434, which was 8 percent higher than it had been in 1990 (adjusted for inflation). But family income was $63,524 when the household head had a two-year-college degree, 10 percent higher than in 1990. A B.A. lifted family income to $85,423, marking a 13 percent increase; an M.A. raised earnings to $101,670, a 17 percent jump. With a professional degree, family income was $147,170, a whopping 24 percent increase from 1990.

It should not be surprising, then, that more high school seniors are seeking to attend college—and more are graduating. But that's not all: Parents and their offspring also assume that future earnings will be higher with a degree from a more selective institution. They figure that future employers will use institutional selectivity as a proxy for the quality of a prospective employee, and that prestigious institutions will offer an abundance of valuable connections to the job market. While the assumption of a direct correlation between selectivity and future earnings is not borne out by research, the tenacity with which it's held says much about how parents view the opportunities and risks faced by young people today. Middle-class and upper-middle-class boomers are determined to do whatever is necessary to increase the chances that their youngsters will do well in the new economy.

The second reason for the lurch toward selectivity has to do with technologies that are knitting together the nation—and the globe. More students than ever are competing nationally (and some internationally) for admission to the same limited set of colleges and universities. Two decades ago, bright high school seniors with good records typically aimed for the best university in their state or region. But rapidly improving technologies of information, transportation, and communication are on their way to creating a single national, and eventually global, market for higher education.

Today, high school students and their parents have an abundance of comparative data about colleges—including standardized ratings such as the annual listings compiled by *U.S. News & World Report*—as well as a flood of information available on the Internet. As a result, bright high school seniors with good grades and test scores are more likely to apply to the big national brands, competing for admission with other students from around the country. Even the sixth graders in the *Times* sample worried about attending a local or regional university. One child intoned, "C is community college, B is state college, A is Ivy League school."

At the same time, and for much the same reason, every major college and university wants a reputation for being among the places that attract the nation's best and brightest. And colleges and universities have access to much more information than they used to about who and where those students are. They are able to communicate with prospects with ever-greater ease.

What does all this mean for us as a society? The danger is that the increasing competition—to be selected and to be selective—will exacerbate the widening inequalities that are raising the stakes in the first place.

There is no single, simple cause of the growing inequality in the United States, but a large part of it relates to supply and demand. In the old economy that dominated the twentieth century, profits and productivity gains depended on making more and more of the same thing. Large numbers of production workers were needed to undertake relatively routine tasks. Those workers did not, in general, require much education. In the new economy of the twenty-first century, by contrast, businesses depend largely on innovation. To stay competitive, they have to generate products and services that are better or cheaper than those of their rivals, and they must innovate faster than their rivals. Thus, demand is growing for people who can spur innovation by identifying and solving new problems or figuring out what clients and customers might need or want.

Even though more young people than ever are attending postsecondary institutions, the demand for workers with the education and skills needed to innovate is rising faster than the supply. By contrast, demand for people with relatively few skills and little education is static or shrinking. And such people are in abundant supply; in fact, many of them can be readily replaced with overseas labor or smart machines. Those trends help explain why the incomes of people with more education have been increasing faster than the incomes of people with less education. As long as the economy is reasonably healthy, less-educated people will continue to have jobs—but their jobs will pay comparatively little.

A society concerned about widening inequality—and its corrosive effects on democracy, social solidarity, and the moral authority of a nation—would logically turn its attention to increasing the supply of people capable of doing the work that the new economy rewards. It would, in particular, do so by broadening access to postsecondary education for children from lower-income families.

Yet almost all the increase in the proportion of eighteen- to twenty-four-year-olds in postsecondary institutions in recent years is attributable to children from middle- and upper-income families. As the economist Thomas Kane has noted, from 1977 to 1993, about 70 percent of eighteen- and nineteen-year-olds from families with incomes in the top quarter attended postsecondary institutions, and that percentage has been rising since then. Slightly more than 50 percent of children from families in the second-highest quartile attended, and 50 percent of children from families in the quartile below that did so. But less than 30 percent of children from families in the bottom quarter enrolled in postsecondary education— a percentage that has been dropping since 1993, even as college enrollments among more affluent students have been rising.

There is a danger that the current competitive rush toward selectivity will make it even less likely that lower-income children will gain access to higher education. That's because college and university administrators have incentives to spend more resources to attract those whom they consider the best students, rather than accommodating more lower-income students whose credentials and test scores do not add to an institution's luster.

Too many colleges and universities are using scarce scholarship resources to lure student stars, who often come from advantaged families and good secondary schools—and who already have every chance of succeeding in life. In fact, an increasing number of institutions are engaging in quiet bidding wars for such students.

The *New York Times* reported that Pittsburgh's Carnegie Mellon University, for example, explicitly reassures star applicants that it will match or surpass any offers they receive from other colleges. "We believe competition among schools is healthy," Carnegie Mellon's admissions director was quoted as saying. "We are trying to encourage dialogue, and we have set aside enough dough to do it." Harvard's admissions materials hint at a similar policy: "We expect that some of our students will have particularly attractive offers from the institutions with new aid programs," it writes to newly admitted students, "and those students should not assume that we will not respond."

Harvard's almost-bottomless endowment allows it to match any bid without skimping on aid to needier students, but that's not the case for most colleges. What's doled out to the stars is almost certainly given at the expense of some needier students who qualify academically, but cannot afford the costs. Across the country, "need-blind" admissions policies are vanishing. "It used to be, providing aid was a charitable operation," Michael S. McPherson, the president of Macalester College, told the *Times*. "Now, it's an investment, like brand management."

A second way that colleges and universities have been pumping up the applicant pool of good students, ratcheting up average SAT scores, and enhancing selectivity is through direct marketing to high schools and families in the middle- and upper-middle-class communities where high achievers can easily be found. An increasing slice of university budgets is now dedicated to mailings, brochures, visits by recruiters to suburban high schools, telephoners, elaborately staged visiting days on campuses, Web pages, and videos. Similarly, money for recruiting minority candidates is often aimed at middle-class African-American and Asian-American families already intent on sending their children to college. Such marketing invites similar responses from competing institutions, in what has become an escalating round of promotion.

Here, too, the result is often less money to finance the much harder job of recruiting high school students from outside the mainstream—diamonds in the rough who could benefit enormously from college but who don't know it because they and their families are too poor, or their high school teachers and administrators too overwhelmed, to become aware of the possibility; or because their performance on standardized tests may not reveal their real promise.

The same competition for the best students is driving many colleges and universities to expand and upgrade student centers, improve campus landscaping, make current dormitories more comfortable, and add other amenities. Administrators argue that they must do so in order to keep up with other colleges in attracting star students and improving institutional rankings. But when such expenditures are passed on to students in the form of higher costs, the consequence is reduced accessibility for needy students who cannot afford the tab.

Alternatively, those expenditures are financed from the proceeds of capital campaigns, which might otherwise be used to expand enrollments and provide more scholarship assistance to the needy. One administrator (again, I should note, not at the institution in which I now teach) explained the logic to me in commendably candid terms: "Our goal is to add more students but to reject more students, If anything, we want a smaller entering class. That way, we look more selective."

Public resources are not being allocated to counter such trends. Many states are starving their public colleges and universities, while cutting the budgets of community colleges (I'm sorry to report that Massachusetts, the cradle of American education, is no exception). From 1988 to 1998, according to the Digest of Education Statistics, the average price of attending a public college or university in America rose 22 percent, after adjusting for inflation (it rose 28 percent at private colleges and universities). Even now, during a recession, tuitions at both public and private universities are rising faster than inflation. That means a lot of children from poor and working-class families can't afford to go.

If we're serious about reversing the larger trend toward widening inequality of income and wealth in the United States—or, at the very least, about slowing it—we need to make it easier, not harder, for children from relatively poor families to gain access to postsecondary education. As boards of trustees and state legislatures debate issues like how to allocate student aid, recruit students, and prioritize capital construction, they need to keep in mind the importance of making higher education available across the economic spectrum.

In light of the nation's widening inequalities of income and wealth, it seems to me that scarce scholarship resources should be reserved for students who need them, rather than for student stars who do not. Colleges should refrain from informally bidding against one another for stars, and from spending significant resources marketing themselves to middle-class families who already are being marketed to death. Resources should be used, instead, to recruit potential students from lower-income families, for whom a college education would be beneficial, but who may not show that by conventional measures. And rather than spending funds on amenities that make campuses more attractive to upper-middle-class children whose families can bear the added costs, colleges should keep a lid on tuition and room and board so that more lower-income kids can afford to attend. Colleges and universities might also consider how to efficiently expand their enrollments to provide better access to more students at lower cost. That could include creative use of the Internet to extend the reach of instructional programs to people who now have little or no access to higher education.

At the same time, and for the same reason, states must make their public colleges, universities, and community colleges a high priority. There's no excuse for short-changing public higher education.

Some people will say that the competitive pressures forcing colleges and universities toward more selectivity cannot be reversed. I accept that some institutional competition is inevitable, even desirable. But I see no inherent reason why the terms of competition must converge on standardized test scores, numerical rankings in such publications as *U.S. News & World Report*, or any such uniform calculus. Institutional success could as well be measured in ways that better respond to the nation's problem of widening inequality—for example, by reference to the proportion of promising new admits from lower-income families.

If the challenge is framed more broadly—as how to help more young people from lower-income families gain the skills they need to succeed in the new economy—other directions may suggest themselves. For example, colleges and universities might offer associate degrees in various technical fields. They might "adopt" high schools in some of the poorer communities in their regions. They could encourage undergraduates to tutor students in those communities and professors to give refresher courses to the high school faculties, and they could aim scholarships and admissions slots at promising students from those schools.

By the same token, state legislatures could expand resources and provide more scholarships for students at state colleges, universities, community colleges, and technical institutes that offer skills that are in demand. And the federal government could expand Pell grants so children from poorer families have the help they need affording college. More states could also grant automatic admission to public universities to in-state students graduating at the tops of their high school classes. Because lower-income students increasingly tend to be concentrated in lower-income communities, such policies would enhance the access of those students to college.

Like the new emphasis on high-stakes exams, the rush toward exclusivity in higher education is exactly the wrong direction to take for a society already becoming less equal, and in which education is the fault line separating winners from losers. We need a new system of universal education that begins with preschool and extends throughout someone's working life—one that strives for excellence but doesn't impose uniformity. In the emerging economy, opportunities abound for young people with originality and flair, for individuals who learn in many different ways. One size doesn't fit all.

CHAPTER FIVE

The Day
I Became a Feminist:
Real Family Values

I lost, by four votes," she said, simply. "I'll be home soon." I must have looked shaken as I put down the phone. Our precocious six-year old, who had been eyeing me, summed up the situation: "They fired Mommy, didn't they?" Sexism had always been something of an abstraction to me. I knew it existed, but I assumed that it was the product of backward and parochial cultures. It might show up in entrenched corporate bureaucracies dominated by old-boy networks, or in ethnic groups governed by male-dominated traditions, or in working-class communities in which Rambo still reigned. But surely no such noxious bias would be found in the overwhelmingly liberal, intellectual, worldly, and high-minded university community that we safely inhabited.

Yet a string of white males had been voted tenure just before her. Most had not written as much as she, nor inspired the same praise from specialists around the nation as had her work. None of their writings had been subjected to the detailed scrutiny—footnote by footnote—to which her colleagues had subjected her latest manuscript. Not one of the male candidates had aroused the degree of anger and bitterness that characterized her tenure decision.

Why? At first I was bewildered. I knew most of the men

who had voted against her. A few I knew to be narrow-minded, one or two I might have suspected of misogyny. But most were thoughtful, intelligent men. They had traveled widely, read widely, had held positions of responsibility and trust. I was sure that they felt they had been fair and impartial in judging her work. They would be appalled at any suggestion of sexual bias.

Gradually, I came to understand. They were applying their standard of scholarship as impartially as they knew how. Yet their standard assumed that the person to whom they applied it had gone through the same training and had the same formative intellectual experiences as they. It assumed further that the person had gained along the way the same understandings of academic discipline, and the same approaches to core problems, as they had gained. In short, their standard was premised on the belief that the people they judged had come to view the modes and purposes of scholarship—of the life of the mind—in the same way they had come to view it.

Through the years my wife has helped me to see the gender biases of these assumptions. Her experiences and understandings, and those of other women scholars, have been shaped by the irrefutable reality of gender. The values and perspectives she brings to bear on the world—and in particular, the world of ideas—are different from theirs, because she has experienced the world differently. In fact, it is the very uniqueness of her female perspective that animates her scholarship, that gives it its originality and intellectual bite. They had applied their standard as impartially as they knew how, but it was a male standard.

Not that they were incapable of appreciating her scholarship simply because they were men: After all, the experts in her field, whose opinions had been solicited during the tenure review, and who had overwhelmingly praised her work, had been male. And the majority of the men on her faculty had voted to grant her tenure; she had failed only to get the necessary two thirds. Presumably, the men who supported her had been able to imagine the life of the mind from a different perspective than their own. They had been able and willing to expand their standard—not to compromise it or to reduce it, but to broaden it to include a woman's way of knowing. I suspect that those who did not, did not care to try.

And why would they not have cared to try? Here again, I was momentarily stumped. Apart from the few diehards, they were kindly men, tolerant men. But perhaps they did not feel that she had invited them to try. Early on, her closest friends on the faculty were a group of young professors who took delight in challenging the sacred cows of prevailing scholarship. Her early articles openly proclaimed a feminist perspective. She had not played at being a good daughter to the older and more traditional men on the faculty, giggling at their jokes and massaging their egos. Nor had she pretended to be one of them, speaking loudly and talking tough. They had no category for her, and to that extent, she had threatened them, made them uncomfortable. So that when it came time for them to try to see the world from her perspective, they chose not to.

Since the vote, she has remained strong and as certain of the worth of her scholarship as before. Many women colleagues, and many men, rallied to her cause. There were student demonstrations. She brought and settled a lawsuit. She was offered a faculty position elsewhere and invested the proceeds of the settlement in an institute to combat domestic violence, where she has found her professional home.

But the experience has shaken me. First came the rage and confusion. Only later came insight into the insidiousness of sexism even in our most enlightened institutions. It has made me wary, in addition, of my own limited perspective—of the countless ways in which I fail to understand my female colleagues and students and their ways of knowing the world.

I have begun to notice small things. A recruiter for a large company calls to ask about a student who is being considered for a job. "Does she plan to have a family?" he inquires, innocently enough. "Is she really—er—serious about a career?" It is not the first time such a question has been put to me about a female student, but it is the first time I hear it clearly, for what it is.

A male colleague is critical of a young woman assistant professor: "She's not assertive enough in the classroom," he confides. "She's too anxious to please—doesn't know her own mind." Then, later, another colleague, about the same young woman: "She's so whiny. I find her very abrasive." It is possible, of course, that she is both diffident and abrasive. But I can't help wondering if these characterizations more accurately reflect how my two colleagues feel about women in general—their mothers, wives, girlfriends—than about this particular young woman.

At a board meeting of a small foundation on which I serve, the lone woman director tries to express doubts about a pending decision. At first, several loquacious men in the group won't give her a chance to speak. When finally she begins to voice her concern, she is repeatedly interrupted. She perseveres and eventually states her objection. But her concern goes unaddressed in the remainder of the meeting, as if she had never raised it. It seems to me that this isn't the first time she was ignored, but it is the first time I noticed.

In my class I present a complex management problem. An organization is rife with dissension. I ask, what steps should the manager take to improve the situation? The answers of my male students are filled with words like "strategy," "conflict," "interests," "claims," "trade-offs," and "rights." My female students use words like "resolution," "relationship," "cooperation," and "loyalty." Have their vocabularies and approaches to problems always been somewhat different, or am I listening now as never before?

The vice president of a corporation that I advise tells me he can't implement one of my recommendations, although he agrees with it. "I have no authority," he explains. "It's not my turf." Later the same day, his assistant vice president tells me that the recommendation can be implemented easily. "It's not formally within our responsibility," she says, offhandedly. "But we'll just make some suggestions here and there, at the right time, to the right folks, and it'll get done." Is the male vice president especially mindful of formal lines of authority and his female assistant especially casual, or do they exemplify differences in how men and women in general approach questions of leadership?

If being a "feminist" means noticing these sorts of things, then I became a feminist the day my wife was denied tenure. But what is my responsibility, as a male feminist, beyond merely noticing? At the least: to remind corporate recruiters that they shouldn't be asking about whether prospective female employees want to have a family; to warn male colleagues about subtle possibilities of sexual bias in their evaluations of female colleagues; to help ensure that women are listened to within otherwise all-male meetings; to support my women students in the classroom, and to give explicit legitimacy to differences in the perceptions and leadership styles of men and women. In other words, just as I seek to educate myself, I must also help educate other men.

This is no small task. The day after the vote on my wife's tenure, I phoned one of her opponents—an old curmudgeon, as arrogant as he is smart. Without the slightest sense of the irony lying in the epithet I chose to hurl at him, I called him a son of a bitch.

My wife will be the first to admit that she's one of the lucky ones. Most working women work long hours at tough jobs for low wages. They sit at the kitchen table late at night trying to figure out how to pay the month's bills. They hope they and their kids stay healthy, because they can't afford to see a doctor. They worry that their golden years will go sour, because the pension they expected disappeared.

They're not on welfare, although some come dangerously close. They don't need a capital-gains tax cut, because most of them don't have very much capital. They are not what the Washington Beltway types like to call a "special interest." They simply work hard—very, very hard—and play by the rules.

They are ordinary Americans holding their family finances together with an unsteady, but ferocious, grip. Since the late 1970s when the wages of men without college degrees started dropping, millions of women have entered the workforce in order to prop up family incomes. But their continuing family role as primary caregivers leads them to move in and out of the workforce, changing jobs many times. Taking time off or working part-time to rear a child or care for an elderly parent often contributes to lower wages, and reduces eligibility for pension benefits or even unemployment insurance. On top of the years of hard work and struggling to care for family and pay the bills, women can pay a steep price when retirement day rolls around.

Here are some facts about working women:

1. Working women are almost half the workforce—sixty million strong.

2. On average, women earn less money than men.

3. Three out of five minimum wage workers are women. More than a third are the sole breadwinners in their households.

4. Nearly two out of three of all working women do not have pension plans.

5. Among those women who are fortunate enough to be earning a pension, the average amount of that pension benefit is only half what men are getting. Once retired, women also tend to live longer than men, meaning what they have saved must last longer and is subject to further years of erosion by inflation.

Allowing the financial security of women to suffer because they have taken responsibility for bearing and rearing their children is wrong for women, wrong for families, and wrong for America.

We're hearing more and more talk about "promoting family values" in America. That's well and good. But some of the people who talk this way are using the term "family values" as a not-so-subtle criticism of working mothers, as well as single mothers, gay couples, new immigrants, or anyone else whose family doesn't resemble the Ozzie and Harriet stereotype.

Another way of talking about "family values" is to focus on the economic burdens that hardworking families are now bearing, and the increasing difficulty of juggling the demands of work and family. If we really want to promote family values in America we need to ease these burdens so more women, and men, can give more time and attention to those they love.

When I traveled around the country as Secretary of Labor, listening to working people and their families, I heard voices that respectfully dissented from the view that the economy was working for everyone. These voices said, "From the perspective of my home the economy isn't doing so great.

At my home, we're still living from paycheck to paycheck. We still can't save for retirement. If I want to earn enough to pay the bills, I can't spend enough time with my kids to raise them right. My job—and our health insurance—is none too secure. And how are we going to pay for college?"

Working families have been taking a pounding. Even though the income of the *average* household increased in the boom years, averages often mask the important details. After all, Shaquille O'Neal and I have an average height of six feet. Households at the top are doing better than ever, so their earnings raise the average. But over the past fifteen years the real wages of most Americans have fallen, and families have had a harder time holding on to a decent standard of living. More and more have lost their grip on the middle class, or their hope for entering the middle class.

Almost 40 percent of all unmarried mothers are earning less than what's needed to lift themselves and their children out of poverty. These mothers' major problem isn't that they're single. Many of them, in fact, are living with men. Some would be better off if they were married, but not all of them would be. Many of the men available to them as potential husbands are earning very little. Some are abusive. These men are among those who have fallen deepest into the post-industrial hole.

The problem of single-parent poverty isn't due to an increased percentage of poor women giving birth to children they cannot afford. The birth rate among all women, including poor women, has dropped. The real problem is that, inevitably, some women have children they can't afford. Some of these women may have behaved carelessly or irresponsibly. Others may have tried to align their family planning with their economic circumstances, but have hit upon bad luck or ill health, or been let down by men they thought they could count on, or slammed by an economy that's become less predictable.

The basic reality is that jobs at the bottom of the income ladder don't pay enough to support a working woman and her children—even if she's living and sharing expenses with a working man who's also near the bottom of the income ladder. Doing away with our national system of welfare in 1996 may have made poor, nonworking mothers less "dependent" on government for handouts, but it hasn't lifted most of them out of poverty. Although the employment rate for single mothers with children has risen since then and the majority are now in paid jobs, poverty rates have barely changed. Most of the welfare poor have now become working poor.

We live in the most economically stratified society in the industrialized world—a nation that is surging toward still greater inequality at an alarming pace. This division itself threatens real family values. It creates fertile soil for the demagogues and conspiracy theorists who often emerge during anxious times.

People who fear for their future naturally cling to what they have and often resist anything that threatens it. People who feel abandoned—by a government that has let them slide or a company that has laid them off—respond to opportunists peddling simplistic explanations for the decline of "family values" and the American Dream. These opportunists tell anxious Americans: It's the fault of immigrants, who are undercutting your wages. Or it's the fault of affirmative action programs, which are letting undeserving others steal your jobs. Or it's the fault of government bureaucrats, who are wasting your tax dollars. Or it's the fault of single mothers on welfare, who are having kids instead of going to work.

But if you listen closely to what these prophets of blame actually propose, you realize their solutions have nothing to do with real families or with real values. In fact, they want to make it even harder for families to make it on their own.

At the very moment our children need nourishment for their bodies and their minds so they can become full and productive citizens of the future, these prophets of blame want to cut school lunches and Head Start.

Exactly when working families need help looking after their children, these blame-mongers oppose affordable child care and paid family leave.

At the very moment working Americans are toiling longer hours for less money, they want to cut the Earned Income Tax Credit to pay for tax breaks for the wealthy.

They demonize people on welfare while doing nothing to end corporate welfare.

At the very time so many Americans need new skills for better jobs, they want to make it harder to get college loans and job training.

Their strategy is simple: Divide and conquer. Ignore the real problems, get anxious people scared and mad at each other. You could even call it class warfare. And we all know it's worked before.

In every era, there are cowards and bullies who try to advance their pathetic causes by using the blunt club of rage rather than the sharp scalpel of reason. Cowards need someone to pick on. I know that from personal experience. When I was a boy, I was smaller than the rest of the kids—and many times I was teased and taunted.

I remember summers in a small town in upstate New York, and I remember a boy who was a few years older than me, a boy named Mickey, who protected me from bullying and gave me some very precious advice. He told me that the bullies could not really hurt me if I was stronger inside than they were inside. He told me that brutish anger is no match for calm determination. And although he perished a decade later, his determination did, in the end, triumph. His full name was Michael Schwerner. He was murdered by a cowardly group of racists in June 1964 as he and James Chaney and Andrew Goodman, also murdered, tried to register voters in Mississippi.

The bullies who swagger through America today are more like the bullies Mickey helped me face down than the bullies who killed him. They make our national life uglier and crueler, rather than murderous. Their weapons are words, which they sharpen with mean-spirited sentiments.

"Family values." How sad, really, that those words aren't used today to comfort or to heal, to praise or to unite. They are more often being used to attack and divide. But we must work to win back every syllable, every letter, of those two words. And we must do so not because we seek advantage for some party or victory for some candidate, but because we seek opportunity and hope for all Americans.

A civilized society is also a civilized economy. Even a nation that deeply respects private decisions about the organization of work can, and indeed must, declare some arrangements out of bounds. Nations set standards of decency. In 1938, we declared in the Fair Labor Standards Act that it is not acceptable to exploit child labor and took the first step to ensure that a minimum wage would be provided to workers. In 1940, we declared in the Veterans Reemployment Rights Act that it is not acceptable to strip workers of their jobs while they are meeting their military obligations to their country. In 1964, we declared in Title VII of the Civil Rights Act that it is not acceptable to deny Americans membership in the workforce because of their race, gender, religion, or ethnic origins. In 1993, we passed the Family and Medical Leave Act, granting up to twelve weeks unpaid leave to employees who have to tend to their own serious illness or to care for a child or other family member.

The Family and Medical Leave Act was an important step in the right direction. I'm proud to have been the Secretary of Labor who implemented it. Consider the two overarching reasons for the legislation. First, American workers should not have to choose between jobs and family when a family member needs help. When a family emergency arises—when workers must be home to attend to seriously ill children or parents, or to newborn infants, or even to their own serious illnesses—it is simply unfair to pit continuing employment against tending to vital needs at home.

Second, family leave actually improves productivity. It's only when workers can count on durable links to their workplace that they are able to make their own full commitment to their jobs. The record of hearings on family and medical leave is full of testimonials from some of America's most respected business leaders on the powerful productive advantages of stable workplace relationships, and on the comparatively tiny costs of guaranteeing that those relationships won't be dissolved while workers attend to pressing family obligations or their own convalescence. The assurance that the job will still be there after a worker has returned home after major surgery, the sick child has recovered, or the new baby has been welcomed into the family, fosters a workplace atmosphere of cooperative learning, flexibility, and continuous improvement. Keeping workers is good for business.

We all bear the costs when workers are forced to choose between keeping their jobs and meeting their personal and family obligations. When they sacrifice their jobs, we all have to pay more for unemployment compensation, retraining, and the rest of the remaining safety net for Americans shaken loose from the productive system. When they ignore their own health needs or their family obligations in order to keep their jobs, we all have to pay more for social services and medical care as neglected family problems worsen.

So what does promoting family values really mean?

It means prohibiting discrimination against someone because she is a woman, or wants to raise a family, or has to attend to family needs.

It means taking the next step on Family and Medical Leave, and giving *paid* leave to employees who must take some time off to care for a child or elderly relative.

It means ensuring affordable child care and elder care.

It means automatically raising the minimum wage when inflation reduces the value of the dollar.

It means expanding the Earned Income Tax Credit and putting more money back in the pockets of millions of working families with modest incomes.

It means making unemployment insurance available to anyone who loses a job—regardless of how long she had held the particular job she lost.

It means helping people save for their retirement by expanding pension coverage—broadening eligibility thresholds to enable more part-timers and in-and-outers to accumulate pensions. And in order to prevent any repetition of what happened to the employees of Enron, making sure that workers don't have to invest more than a small fraction—

say 10 percent —of their 401(k) savings in the company they work for, and are allowed to sell their stock whenever they wish.

That's what "family values" means. It is an agenda centered on home economics.

Some politicians who speak fervently of family values leave out home economics. They talk passionately about the breakdown of American homes, but they neglect to mention the breakdown of family incomes.

The true test of a society is its willingness to face up to its core problems—not to deny them, not to project them on to scapegoats, not to be diverted by issues of the moment, and not to become easily discouraged when the problems require patience and sacrifice—but to work at them with steadfast commitment.

Self-righteous talk is easy and it's cheap. Securing people good jobs is neither easy nor cheap.

We must explain what "family values" really mean, and not be cowed by the crowd that thinks it has a copyright on those precious words. Let's have a great debate about family values. But let's have it on our terms.

We honor family values every time children have a safe place to grow when their parents are at work. We honor family values every time we secure a working family's pension. We honor family values every time we teach a child to learn. We honor family values every time we move a young mother from welfare to work, or help a worker get better skills, or help someone who has lost a job find a new one. And, yes, we honor family values when all of us become feminists; when we recognize the additional burdens women have traditionally borne at work and at home because of their gender, and try to share more equally the rewards of work and the responsibility of home.

CHAPTER SIX

The Long View: A Decent Working Society

All of us have been changed by what occurred September 11, 2001, the worst act of terrorism in our nation's history. Thousands lost their lives. Millions of us lost our innocence. The horror and pain of it—and the accompanying fear—have caused many of us to ask ourselves a basic question: What are we willing to sacrifice so our children can grow up in a better world? Not since John F. Kennedy raised the question have so many of us wondered what we can do for our country.

Most Americans now realize national security is more than simply a matter of building weapons. Real security begins with the strength of our society. Real patriotism starts with a knowledge we're all in the same boat. Our children's future security depends on the bonds we create and sustain today.

Most of all, we're bound together by common ideals. They aren't just noble ideals about freedom and justice. They're also practical principles about what we owe and expect from one another as members of the same society.

They involve our obligation to work, if we can, be good parents to our children, and be caring members of our communities. But they also involve the mutual obligations of those who hire us. And the responsibilities of all of us to every other member of our society who plays by these rules. They are "kitchen-table" principles—in the sense that most of us live them, or at least aspire to live them, every day.

To summarize: First, as companies do better, their employees should, too. Profitable businesses should do everything possible to keep people employed instead of laying them off. They should provide employees with health and retirement benefits, and help them upgrade their skills.

Second, jobs should pay enough to lift a family out of poverty. This requires an adequate minimum wage indexed to inflation, coupled with a sufficiently generous earned-income tax credit. Poorer families can also be encouraged to save through plans matching the dollars they put away with public dollars or refundable tax credits. And when the job falls through or isn't available, families need to be able to count on adequate income assistance and health care. Unemployment insurance (designed for an old economy where people were laid of temporarily during downturns and then got the old job back again on the upturn) should be replaced by a re-employment system emphasizing new skills for new jobs.

Third, all of us should have full opportunity to make the most of our God-given talents and abilities. That means good care and early-childhood education for all children, high-quality K through 14 (including universal access to at least two years of public education beyond today's high school), affordable colleges and universities, and ample opportunities for lifelong learning. It also means no one should be discriminated against because of gender, race, ethnicity, or sexual orientation.

These principles aren't "liberal" or "conservative." They're at the moral core of America. They're as important to economic growth as they are to social equity. Businesses can't be productive without skilled and healthy workers. Companies can't do well over the long term unless they act responsibly toward their employees and communities. Consumers won't buy much unless they feel some economic security about the future. Our economy can be successful only if all people have the chance to make the most of their abilities.

Most Americans support these principles because they define a decent working society. A few years ago, when I was Secretary of Labor, I helped fight for an increase in the minimum wage. Republicans controlled both houses of Congress. Dick Armey, the majority leader of the House, said he'd oppose a minimum-wage increase "with every fiber of my being." Dick Armey is a big man. He's got a lot of fibers in his being. But we won that fight anyway. Why? Because the vast majority of Americans thought raising the minimum wage was the fair and decent thing to do. It hadn't been raised in years. Even though 95 percent of these Americans got no benefit from raising it—and some may even have had to pay a few pennies more for the goods or services they bought— they supported the move. It was right.

Now, after September 11, there's even a stronger determination to do what's right by one another.

* * *

113

Cynics don't believe the global economy allows us to live in a decent society. They say that global capital undermines any social contract. They're wrong. It's true that investment capital now sloshes around the world to wherever it can get the highest return. But that doesn't mean we have to compromise our core principles in order to attract it.

Every city or town, every state, every region—indeed, every nation—really has two choices about how to attract global capital. One choice is to become so inexpensive that global capital is lured by the low cost of doing business: Wages are rock bottom. Workers get no health or retirement benefits. Safety regulations don't exist or are barely enforced. Companies are free to pollute. Taxes are waived.

This low-cost strategy may indeed attract global capital and create a lot of jobs. But they'll be lousy jobs. Families will be condemned to a low standard of living. The environment will be degraded. And the entire economy will be precarious because there will always be somewhere else on the globe where the costs are even lower. After all, textile companies abandoned New England for North and South Carolina in the early twentieth century. By the late twentieth century they were abandoning the Carolinas for Mexico and Asia.

The other choice is to lure global capital by becoming so productive that even though wages may be high, benefits generous, and regulations costly, capital is eager to come because workers are able to produce more and better products. They can identify and solve new problems, create ever more efficient ways of doing things, and respond to customer needs more quickly and deftly.

Why, under this second scenario, are people more productive? Because they're well educated and because they and their families are in good health. They're also productive because they're able to commute to and from work efficiently, because they can confidently leave their young children in good care, and because all can make full use of their talents and abilities regardless of race, gender, or sexual orientation.

This highly productive society will attract global capital and generate a lot of jobs. But unlike the low-cost alternative, these jobs will be good ones, allowing a high standard of living. And unlike the low-cost alternative, this high-productivity strategy is completely consistent with the core principles of a decent working society.

But to become a highly productive society, we have to change our thinking about the role of government. We've become so accustomed to thinking about education, health care, child care, and public transportation as government *spending* that we don't see the obvious: In the new global economy where financial capital is footloose, these are critical public *investments*. They mark the only path to a sustained and shared prosperity. Failure to make them—and make them wisely—condemns a society to a steadily declining standard of living. The same is true for regulations protecting worker safety, guarding the environment, and preventing discrimination. These, too, are investments in our future.

In other words, making these investments is both an ethical imperative and an economic necessity.

The current administration in Washington doesn't share this understanding. The President aims to spend billions on military hardware and to award huge tax breaks to global corporations and wealthy individuals. The predictable result is a budget squeeze so tight there's hardly any money left for critical public investments.

State governments, already hard-pressed by the economic slowdown, can't begin to make up the difference. Some misguided governors are doing even more damage by cutting back at the state level on current inadequate levels of public investment.

Even if a large military buildup is the only way to deal with the threat of global terrorism—a dubious proposition in light of the growing numbers around the world succumbing to poverty, disease, and hunger, on which terrorism thrives —there's no justification for huge tax breaks to corporations and the wealthy as a means toward a stronger economy. "Trickle-down" economics is a semireligious faith resting on the flawed idea that corporations and rich individuals, blessed with extra riches, will invest more of their money and spur economic growth. But in the global economy investment dollars travel the world in search of the highest return. Any extra dollars big corporations and wealthy individuals might invest are instantly pooled with the money of other global investors. This vast pool of global capital will go to low-cost producers around the world and to highly productive ones. But there's no particular reason to suppose it will stay in America.

Furthermore, the critical issue isn't whether America attracts global capital. It's on what terms we attract it. We can enjoy a high standard of living only if we attract global capital based on our high productivity. And high productivity depends critically on public investments and sensible regulations.

Call it "bubble-up" economics. Rather than award large tax breaks to corporations and wealthy individuals, we ought to invest in what's uniquely within our nation's borders—our people. Our knowledge and skills, our health, and our ability to work productively together are the key assets on which our future standard of living depends.

I'm not talking about just some of us. I'm talking about *all* of us. Turning our backs on anyone—poor kids, people with disabilities, people of color, ethnic minorities, women—isn't only unjust, it's also economically wasteful. It reduces our productive potential. It causes all of us to be poorer than we would be otherwise.

So why are we allowing the Bush administration to take us so blatantly in the wrong direction? The President appeals for sacrifice but then awards a mind-numbing tax cut to those who need it least, while imposing ever-greater burdens on the neediest among us. He talks about national security but undermines the economic security of American families.

He asks us to join together in common purpose but then gives energy companies freedom to pollute, gives airline companies massive bailouts without a penny for the thousands of airline employees who lose their jobs, proposes to restore the three-martini tax-deductible lunch beloved by Washington lobbyists, and wants to eliminate the corporate

Alternative Minimum Tax enacted fifteen years ago to make sure big companies don't exploit so many tax loopholes they avoid paying taxes altogether. And he wants to eliminate it *retroactively* so the big companies can get back whatever minimum taxes they paid over the past fifteen years.

True patriots should not accept any of this.

There are three recurrent obstacles to progressive reform. Overcome these obstacles and positive change is possible; leave any one standing and regressive forces hold sway.

The first obstacle is denial. Some people say that we have no real problems on the home front. They deny that a growing number of Americans—some 40 million at last count—lack health insurance. They refuse to acknowledge that many of our schools are literally falling apart, that an ever-larger proportion of working parents cannot afford safe and stimulating child care for their youngsters while they are at work, or long-term care for their elderly parents, and that a large number of workers lack the skills they need to move to better jobs. They don't recognize that almost a fifth of our nation's children are in poverty, that the ranks of the homeless are growing, and that the income and wealth gap between rich and poor continues to widen.

The second obstacle is escapism: Some people may accept these realities but choose to ignore them. After all, they and their families are doing OK. They've convinced themselves they don't have to deal with those who are barely holding on, or are in free fall. It seems easier to retreat into condos, gated communities, office parks, and suburban malls—and assume that the larger problems are other people's concerns.

The third obstacle—and the worst of all—is resignation. Even if they acknowledge what's happening and don't try to escape from it, some people have grown cynical about the possibility of changing things for the better. Maybe they tried when they were younger and idealistic, but grew discouraged. Maybe they burnt out trying to make a difference. Or they concluded that the task is just too large, the regressive forces in society just too powerful. Others have simply given up on all forms of politics. They've decided politics is inherently corrupt.

Denial, escapism, and resignation are not new responses to social challenges. They have always been the main barriers to progressive change. Historically, reform has occurred only when they are surmounted.

One such period occurred at the start of the industrial era, in the latter decades of the nineteenth and in the early twentieth century. Then Americans faced an economic transition roughly comparable to the one we face today. Within a short period America had been transformed into a society of large cities teeming with immigrants and the poor, of giant corporations and trusts, and of widening disparities of income and wealth.

The nation responded. Appalled by sweatshops, people demanded laws setting minimum wages and maximum hours, and guarding worker health and safety. Other laws recognized unions and required collective bargaining. The "high school movement" extended free public schooling through twelfth grade, and then added kindergartens. Antitrust laws were passed and enforced against the combinations. Congress enacted a progressive federal income tax and several states enacted the first systems of social insurance against injuries on the job and unemployment.

The new global economy into which we are entering requires new reforms that are no less comprehensive. The ideas I've advanced in this book are points of departure.

How to overcome denial, escapism, and resignation? How to create new politics premised on "bubble-up" economics, public investment, and social equity? I'll give you a one-word answer: leadership. Leadership is the ability to get people to focus on issues they'd rather not pay attention to. Leadership is the art of overcoming denial, escapism, and resignation.

To be a leader you don't have to have formal authority. You don't need to be a president, governor, mayor, or head of a major corporation or foundation. You can exert leadership from almost anywhere. Maybe you're already a leader. You exert leadership by helping people see what must be done. You focus their attention on the work at hand. You make sure they understand that the problem or challenge exists; they can't deny it. You show them why they must be involved in solving it; they cannot escape from it. And you give them the courage and confidence to believe that it can be solved; you don't allow them to hide behind cynicism and resignation. We—you and I—can create a decent working society, if we exert the leadership that's required.

It's the right time. A new spirit is taking hold in America. Until recently, the presumed goal was simply to strike it rich —win big in the stock market, buy your own South Sea island or private jet, have a bigger house than your neighbor, look out for Number One. We didn't pay much attention to the widening disparities of income, wealth, and opportunity. We didn't much notice the depths of poverty here at home and around the world. We overlooked the stresses on families trying to balance the bills while paying for child care, health care, elder care, college for the kids.

We thought our economy was unstoppable. Then the bubble burst. We thought we were invulnerable. Then terrorists struck.

Most of all, we forgot, temporarily, what we once knew: We're all in this together. Our common wealth lies not in the fatness of our individual wallets but in the productivity of every one of us. Our common strength lies not in our bombs, but in our bonds.